NORDERNEY DIARY

Peter Bialobrzeski

November 22 – November 28, 2019

Hartmann books

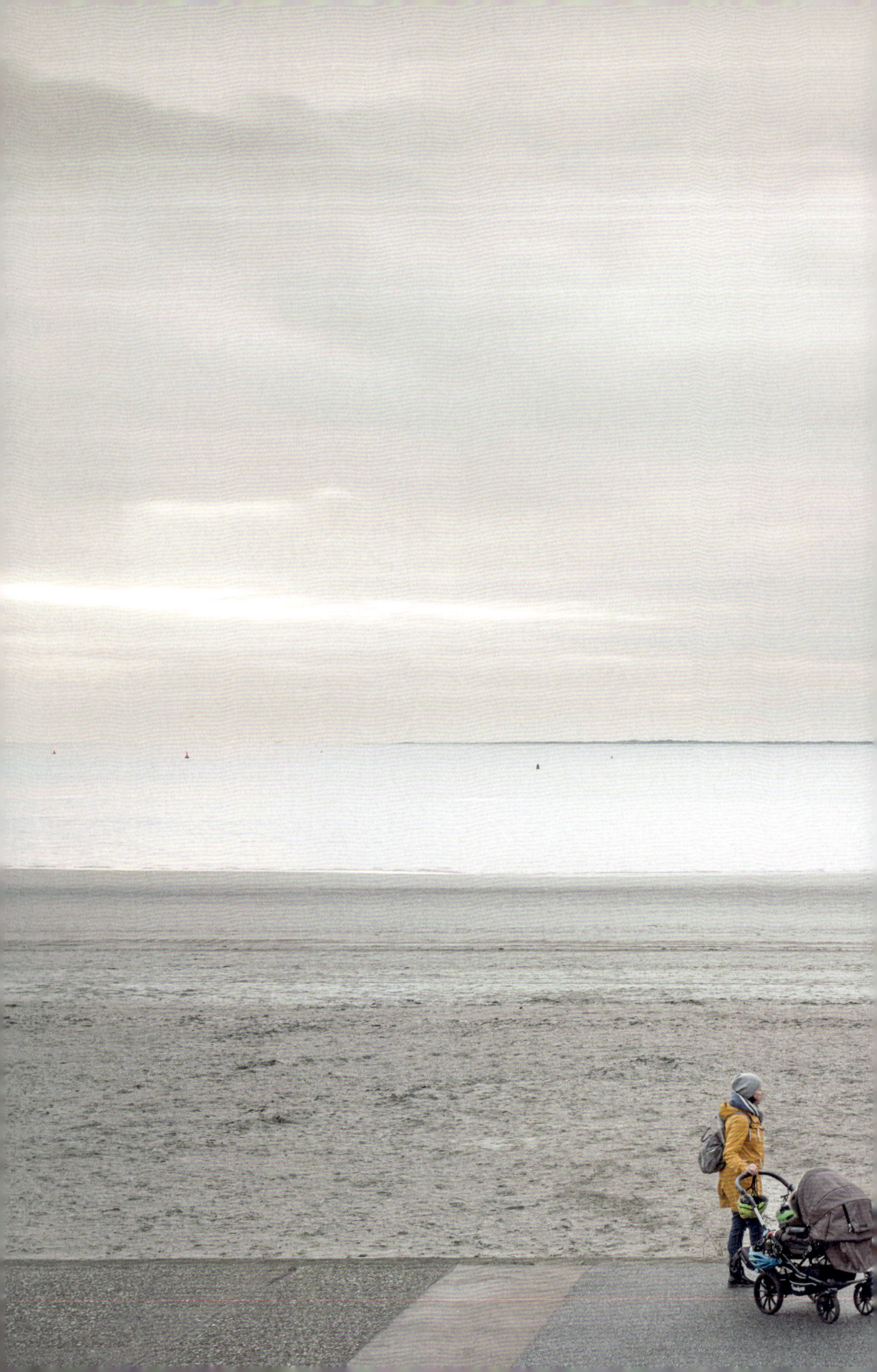

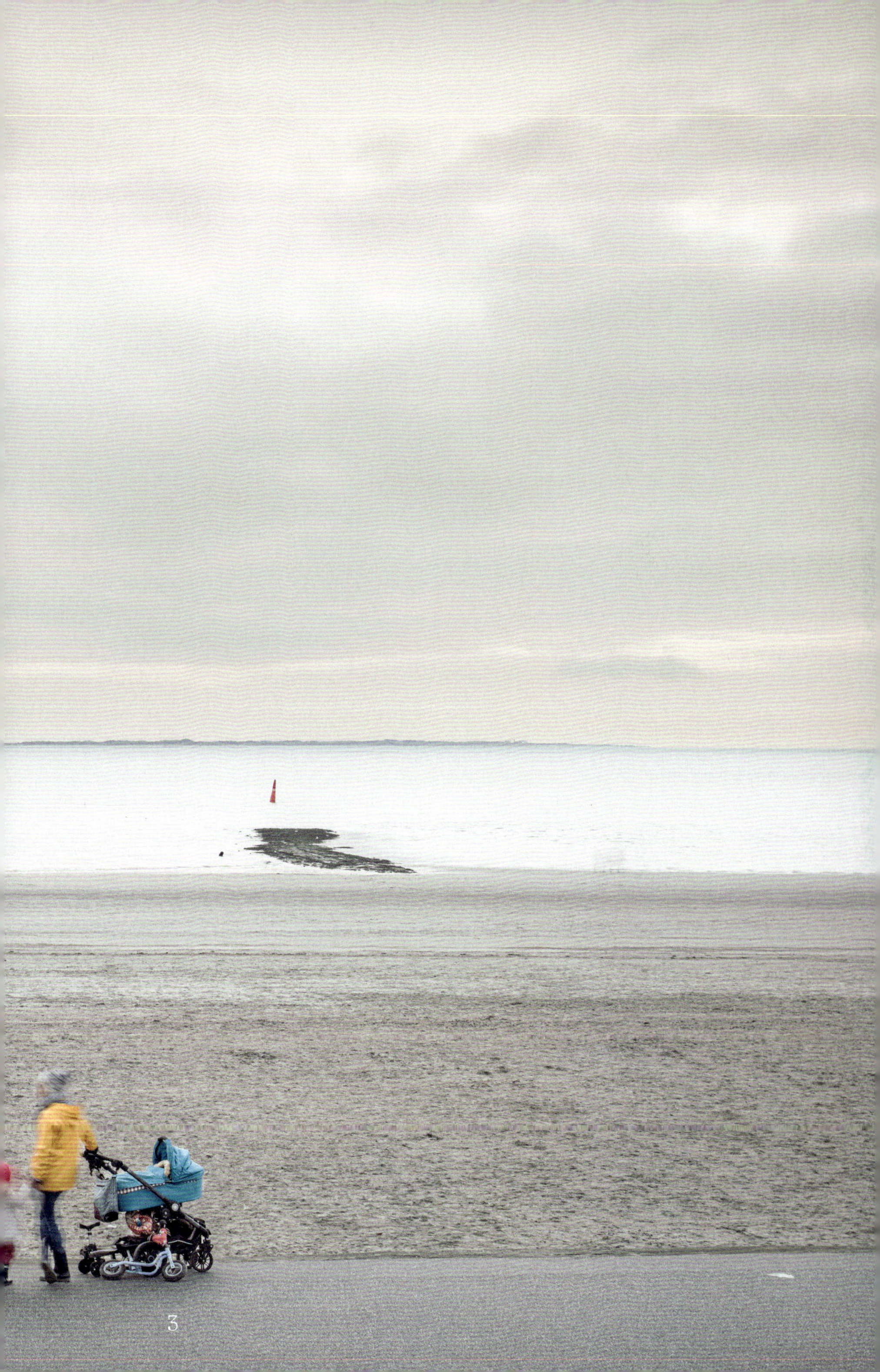

NORDERNEY DIARY
Peter Bialobrzeski

→November 22, 2019 As if the gods had mercy, the sky opens after a shitty, rainy week on the mainland, and a soft light transforms the island ferry into a vehicle for a brighter week ahead. Instead of sky, beach, and sand, a possible new diary appears on the horizon, made up of a skyline of buildings that speak of a late-modernist dream of tourism.
→November 23, 2019 Only the strong winds in the car-free streets of the port of Norderney remind me that I am on an island. The mix of architecture from the late nineteenth century, broken by the atrocities of the 1960s and 1970s, could be found in any East Frisian town along the coast, one might think. These hidden, nineteenth-century architectural gems, however, bear witness to the early days of tourism on the North Sea.
→November 24, 2019 Speaking of tourism: the local paper reports the confession of a thirty-one-year-old drunk who threw a bottle from a "party train" that hit a two-year-old girl on the head. The paper points out that the man was fortunately taken off the train by the police before it reached the island.
→November 25, 2019 The morning is foggy and wet. The North Sea, known for its wind and huge waves, is surprisingly calm for a gray November day. The weekenders have left the island. A guy named Denis Grass, who "designs" T-shirts inspired by the island, makes the front page of the *Norderneyer Badezeitung*. Copyright laws, he tells the journalists, prevent him from mentioning the island directly, but "his heart beats for Norderney." Did I mention that he is not an islander?
→November 26, 2019 Nothing ever happens. Nothing? Every weekday morning, small vans of craftsmen and builders are

the main feature on the streets. Renovations are taking place to build or refurbish the accommodations for the upcoming season. I cannot possibly imagine what it would be like to spend a week here in the summer. The main story in today's local press is the "crimelike-victory" of the *Vull Kraft* team over the *Siedlung* team. This particular sport is played nowhere outside of East Frisia. The locals call it *Bosseln*, best translated as "street bowling"—whatever you may imagine, dear reader.
→November 27, 2019 A center for events, the *Conversationshouse*, cinema, theater, and more, hosts a *Virtual Island Walk*. It is more of a lecture than a walk, given by a retired teacher from Jever, a neighboring town on the Frisian mainland. Tourists can sit comfortably and view digital images of the remote eastern part of the island instead of making the arduous walk IRL.
→November 28, 2019 An unusual sight has been spotted by the editors of my favorite local newspaper: a gray swan has been roaming around downtown Norderney. They wonder if it is looking for a Christmas present for its spouse, reminding readers that swans are known to mate for life. Meanwhile, the neighboring island of Wangerooge is discussing the possibility of getting rid of copper coins because the *Frisian Bank* in Jever has declared it "too expensive" to transport the coins to and from the island. Norderney is proud to announce that an episode of the cult German crime show *Tatort* is currently being filmed on the island. Its topic is illegal real estate activities.

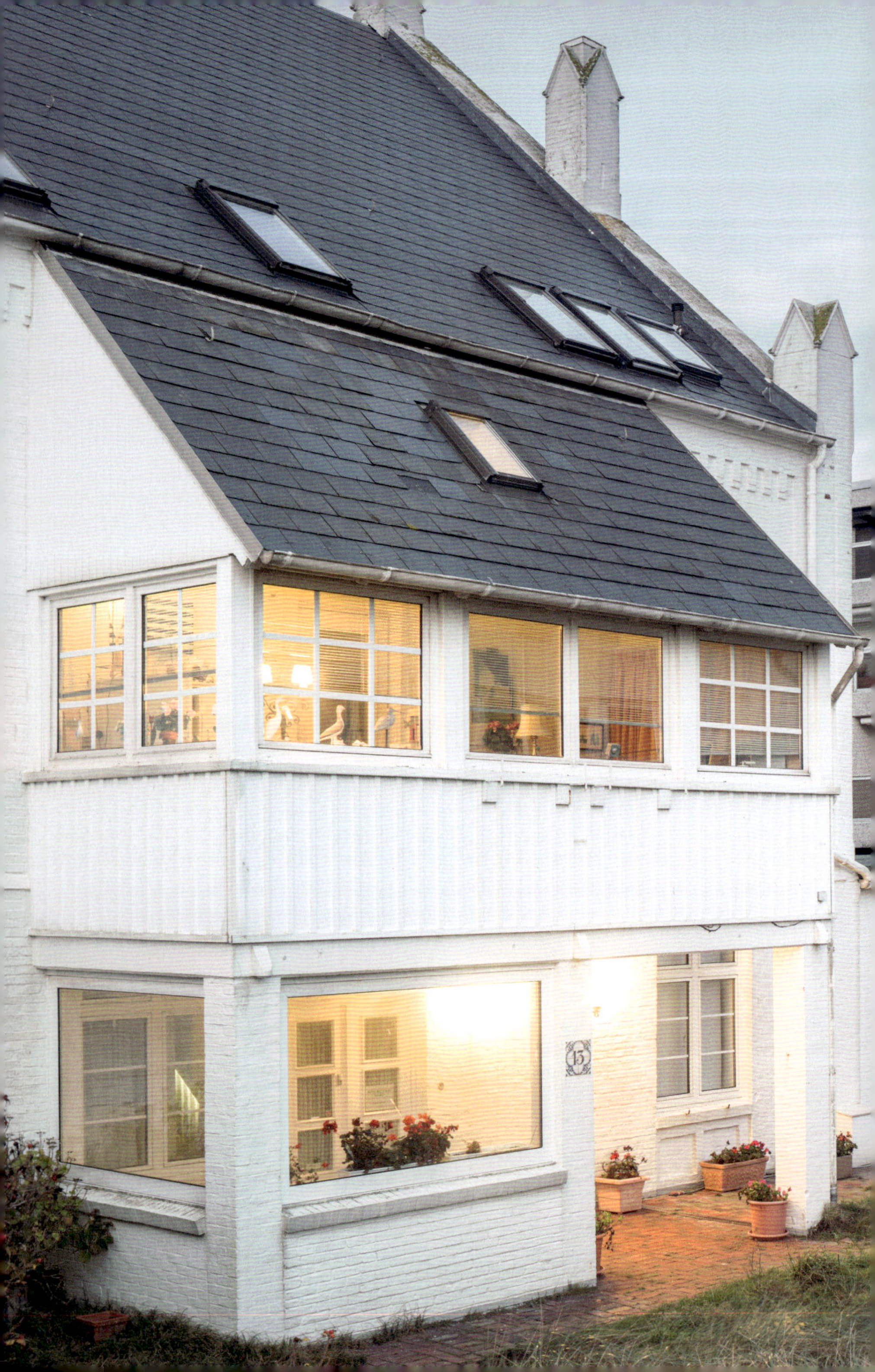
13

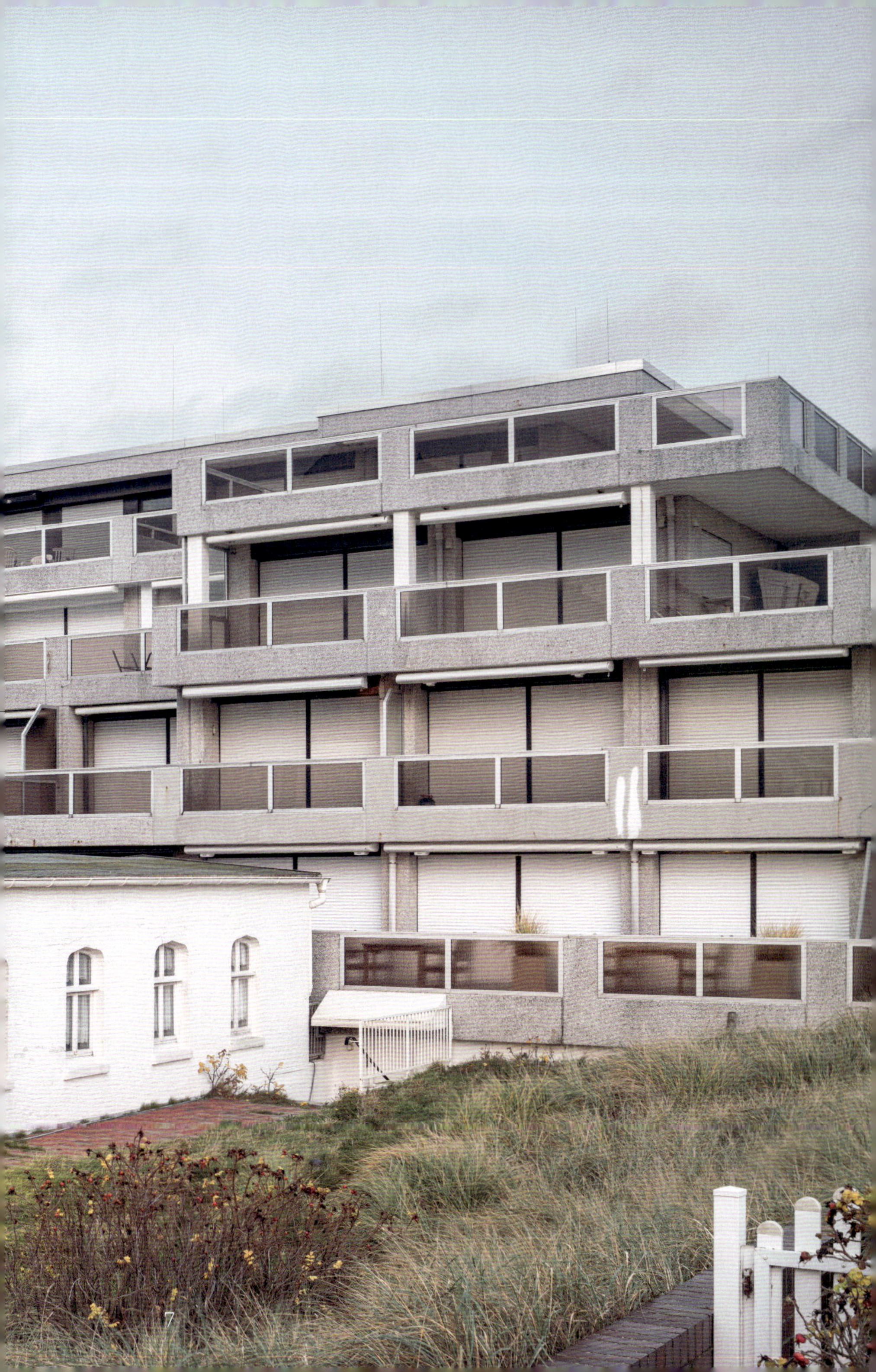

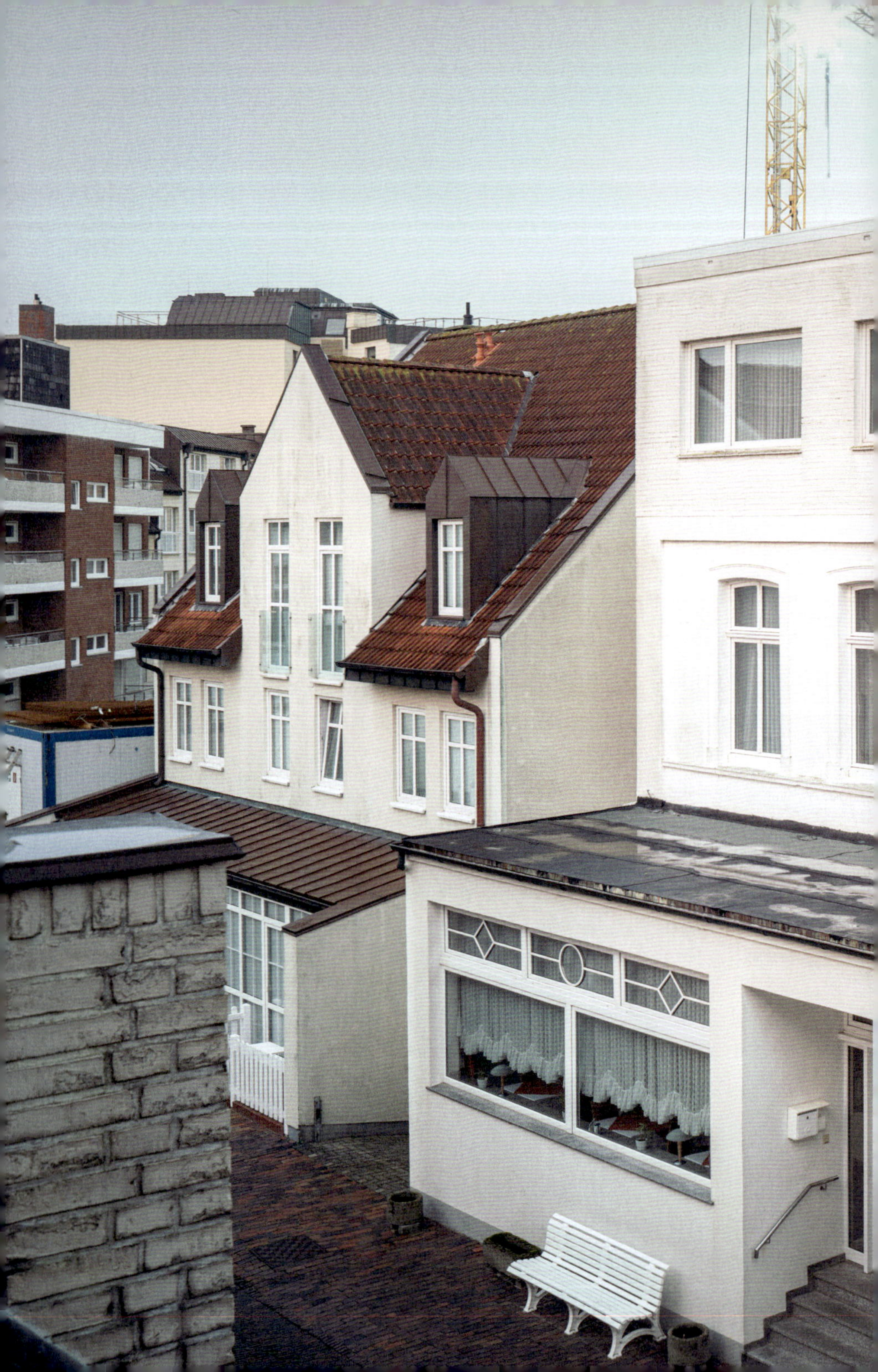

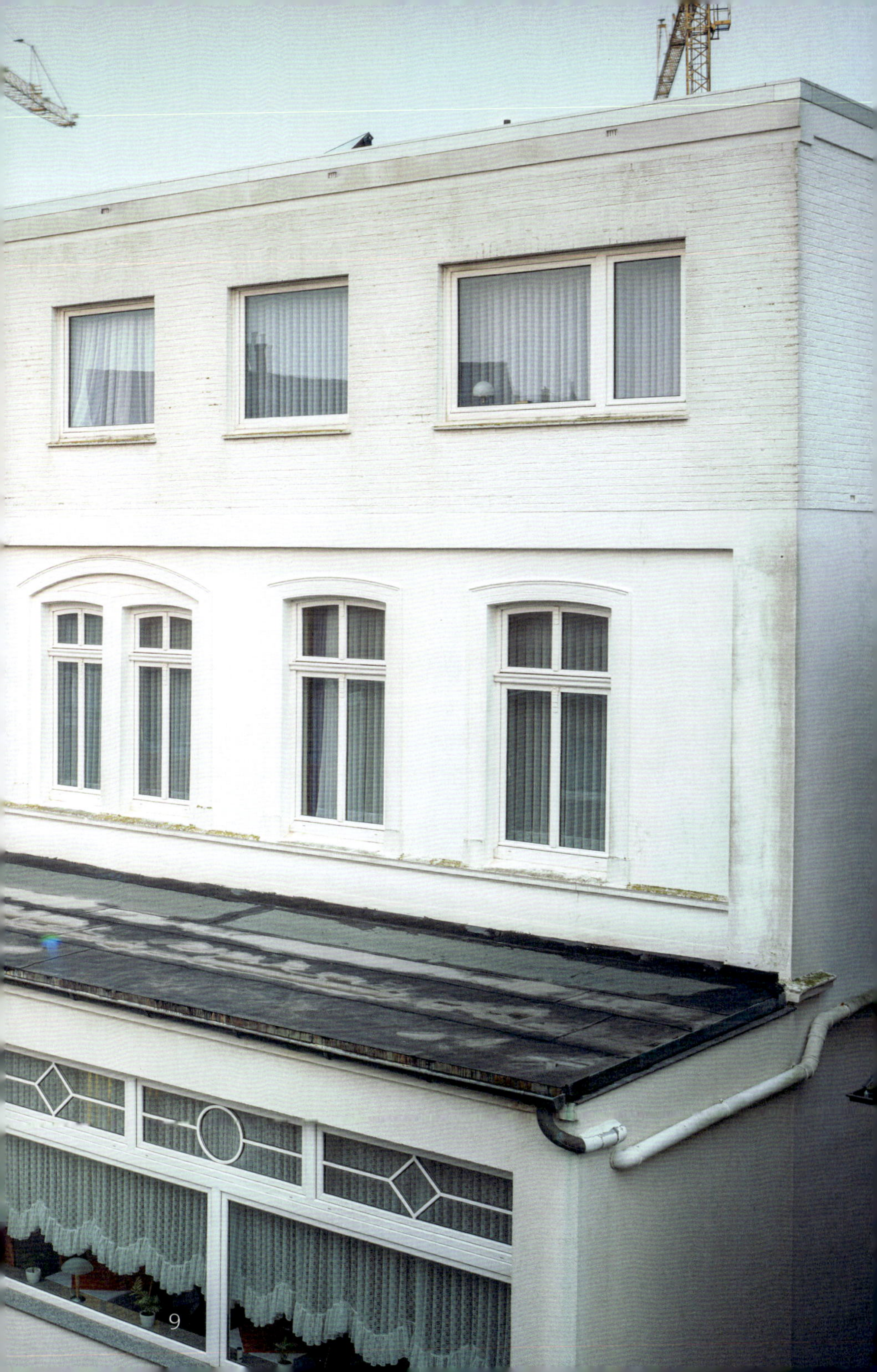

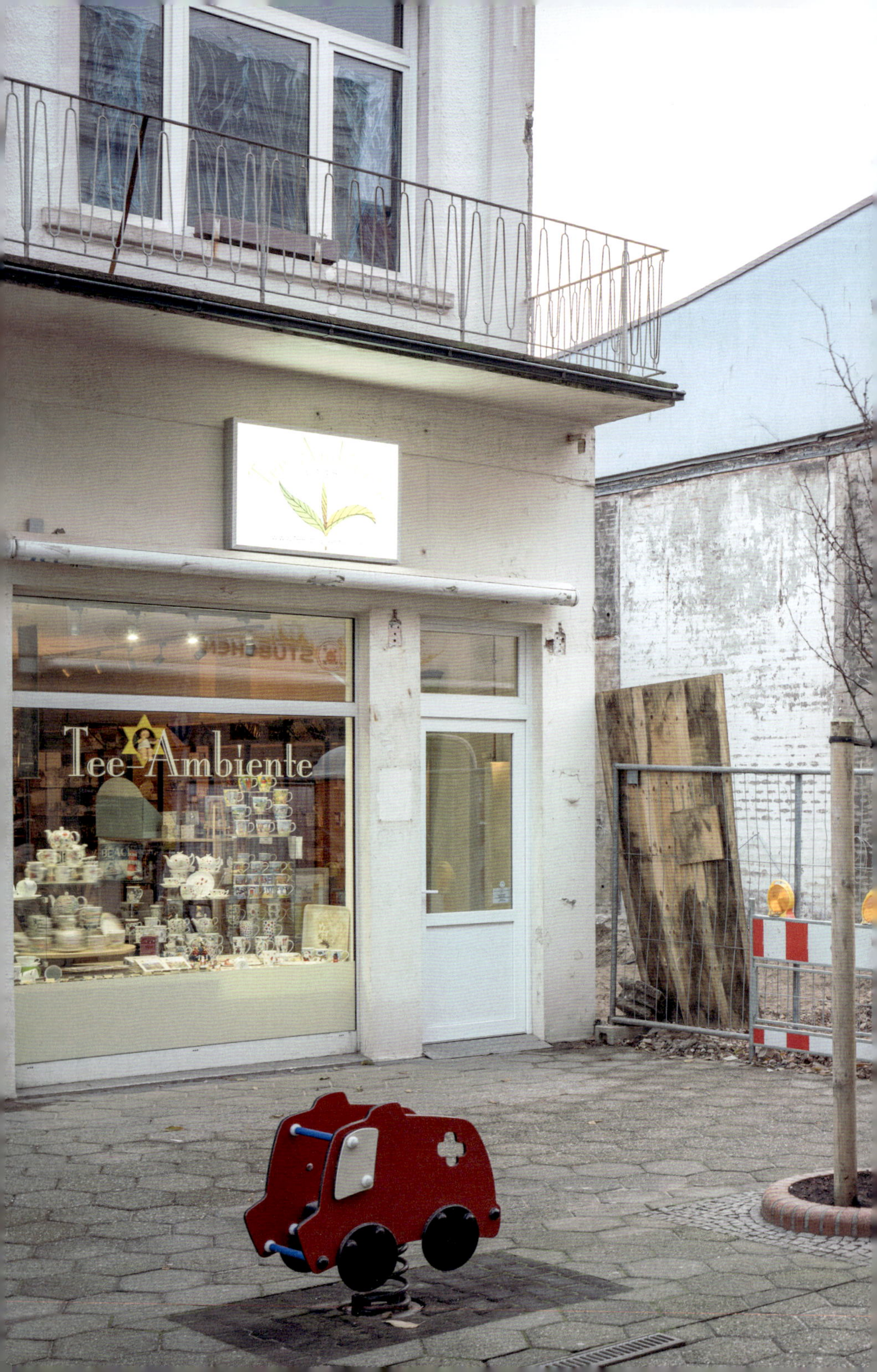
Tee-Ambiente

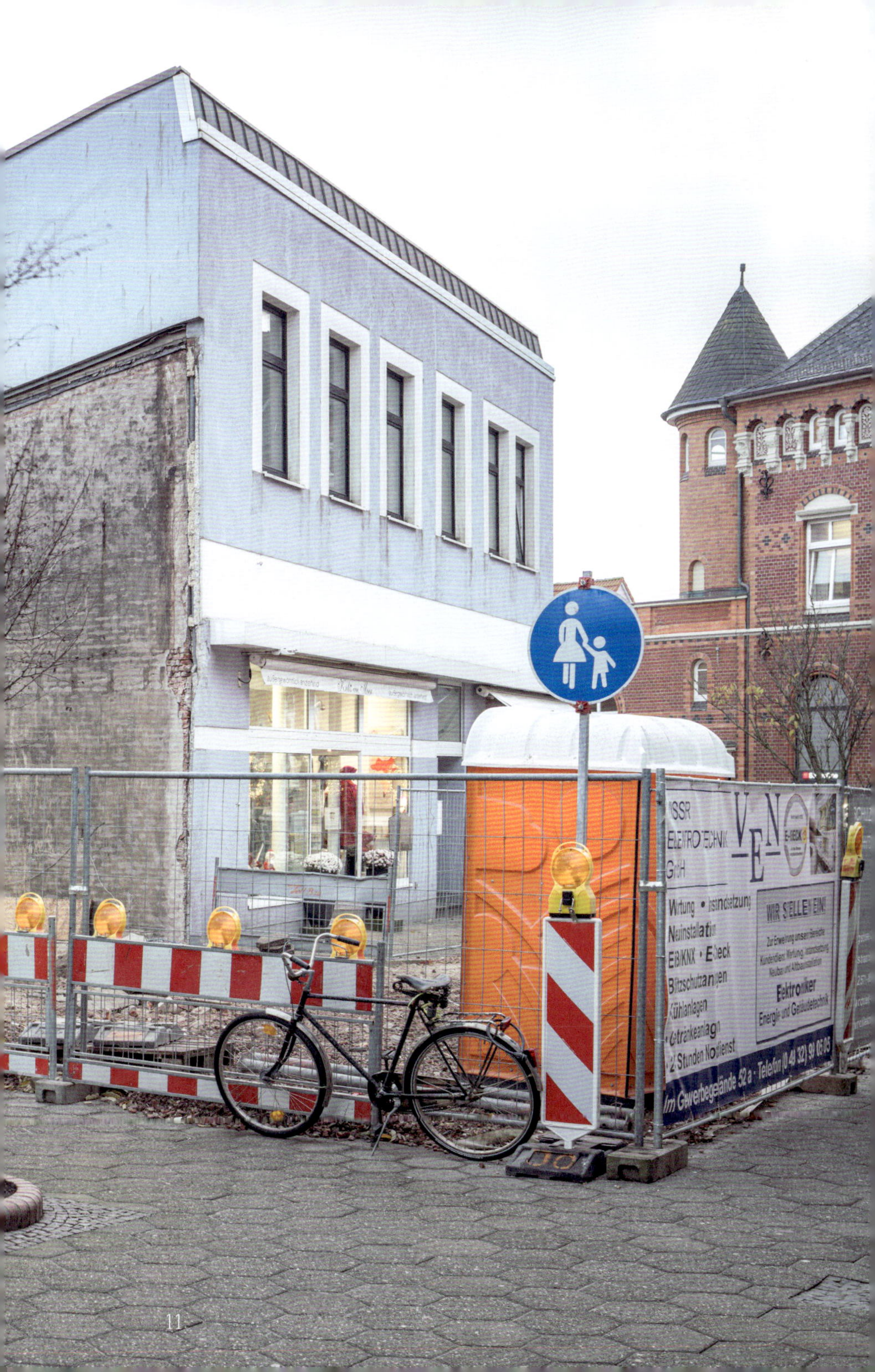
Kühlanlagen
Im Gewerbegelände 52 a

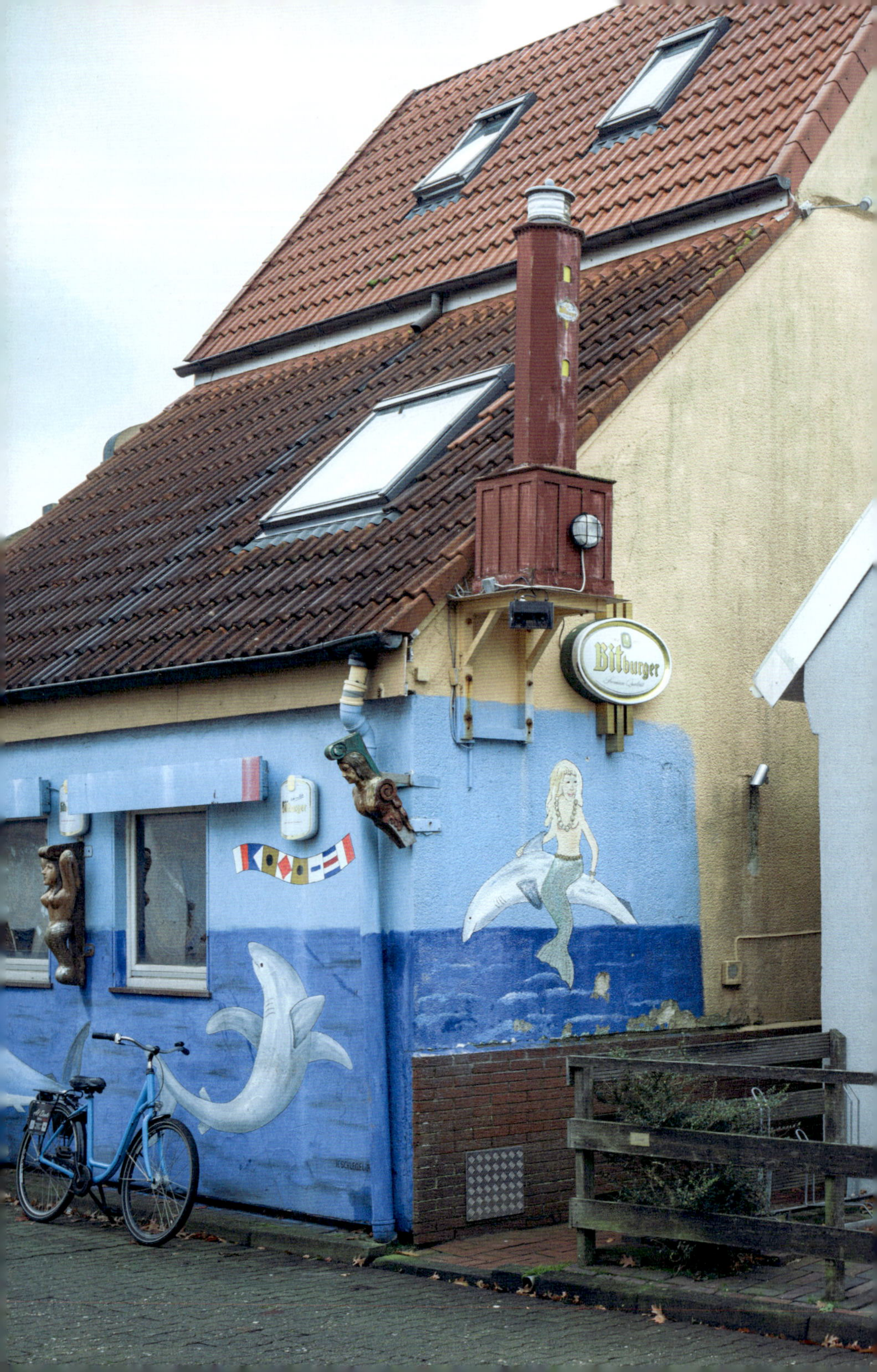
Bitburger

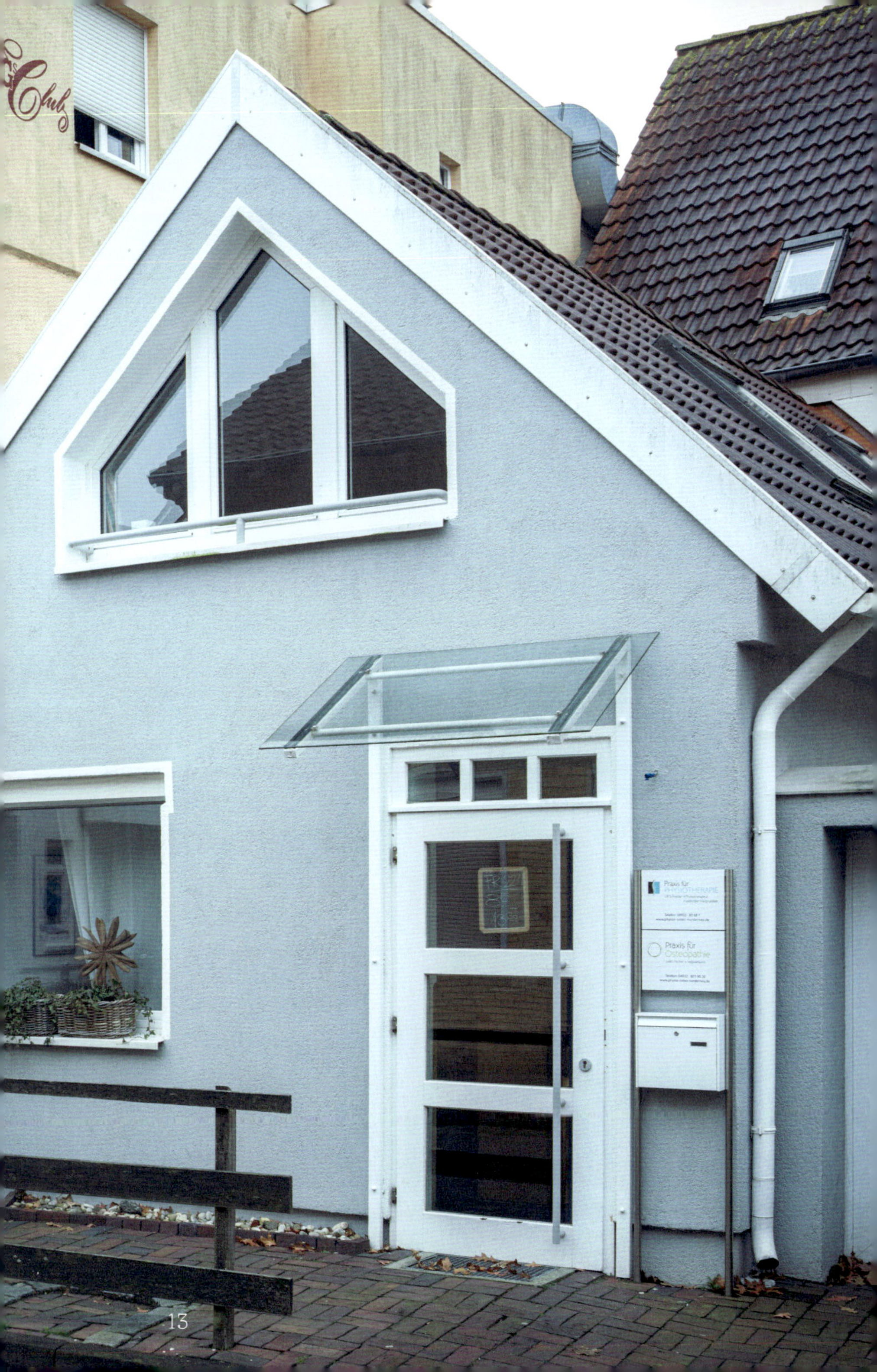
Praxis für
PHYSIOTHERAPIE
Praxis für
Osteopathie

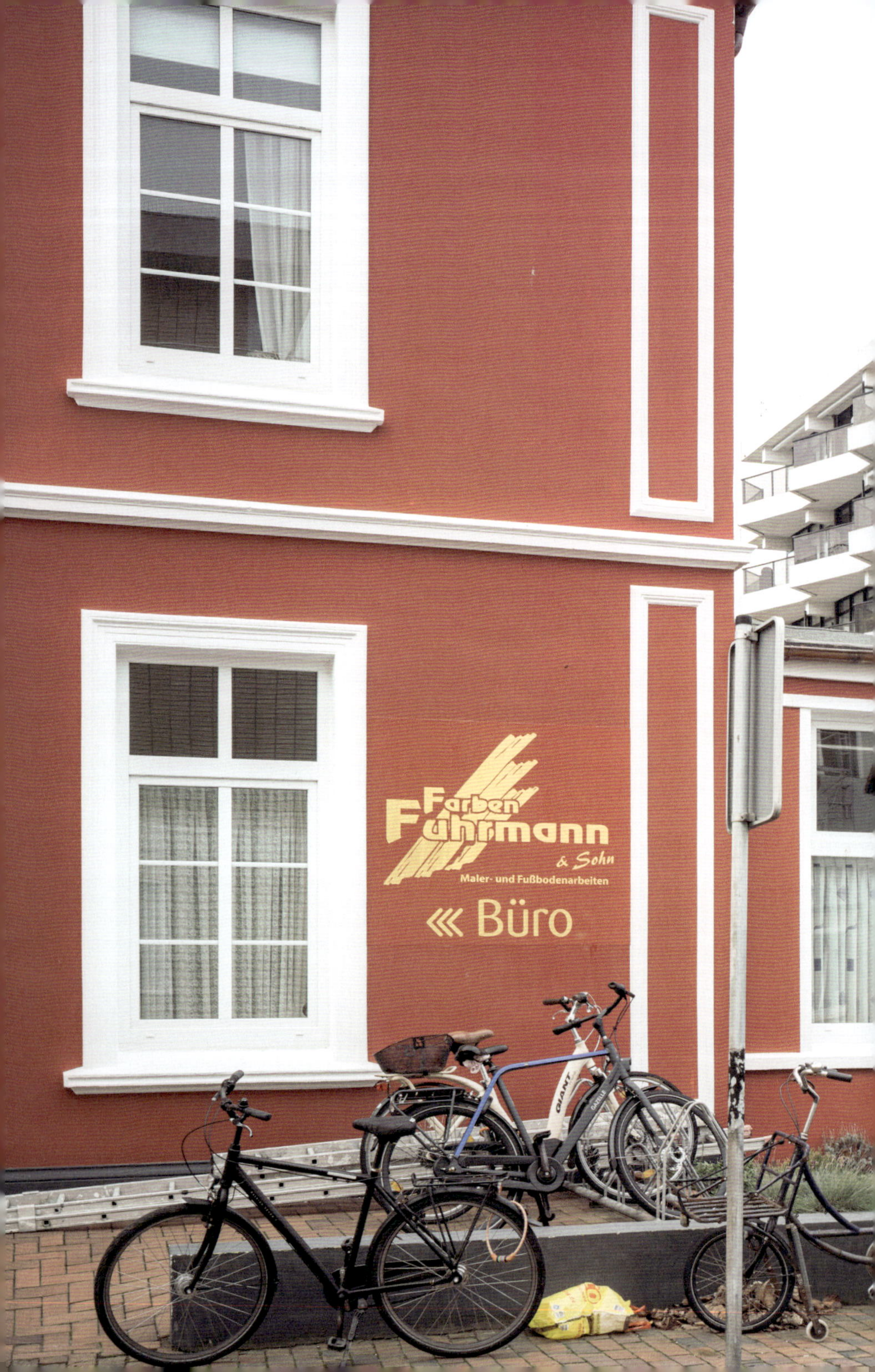
Farben
Fuhrmann
& Sohn
Maler- und Fußbodenarbeiten
Büro

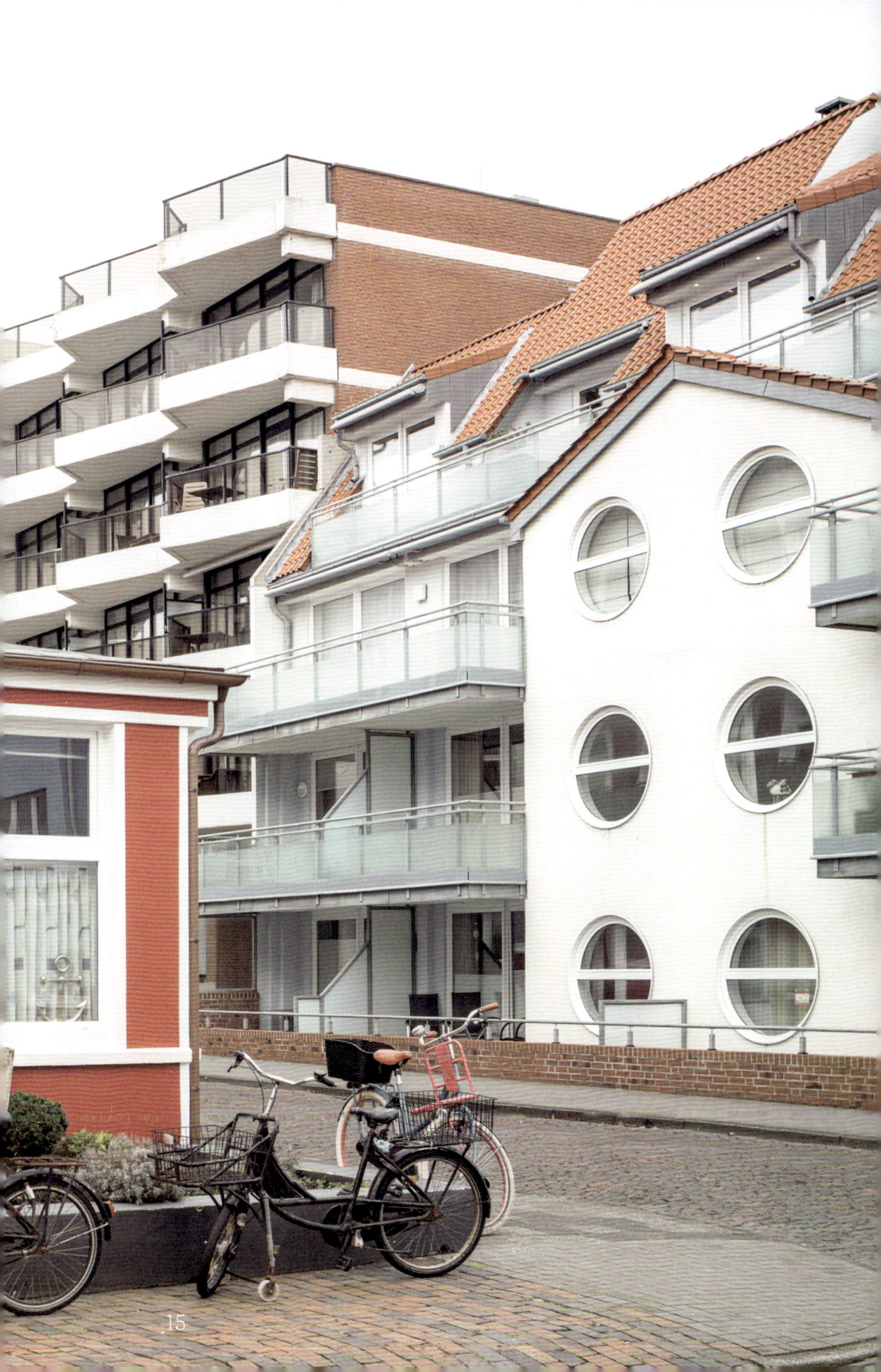

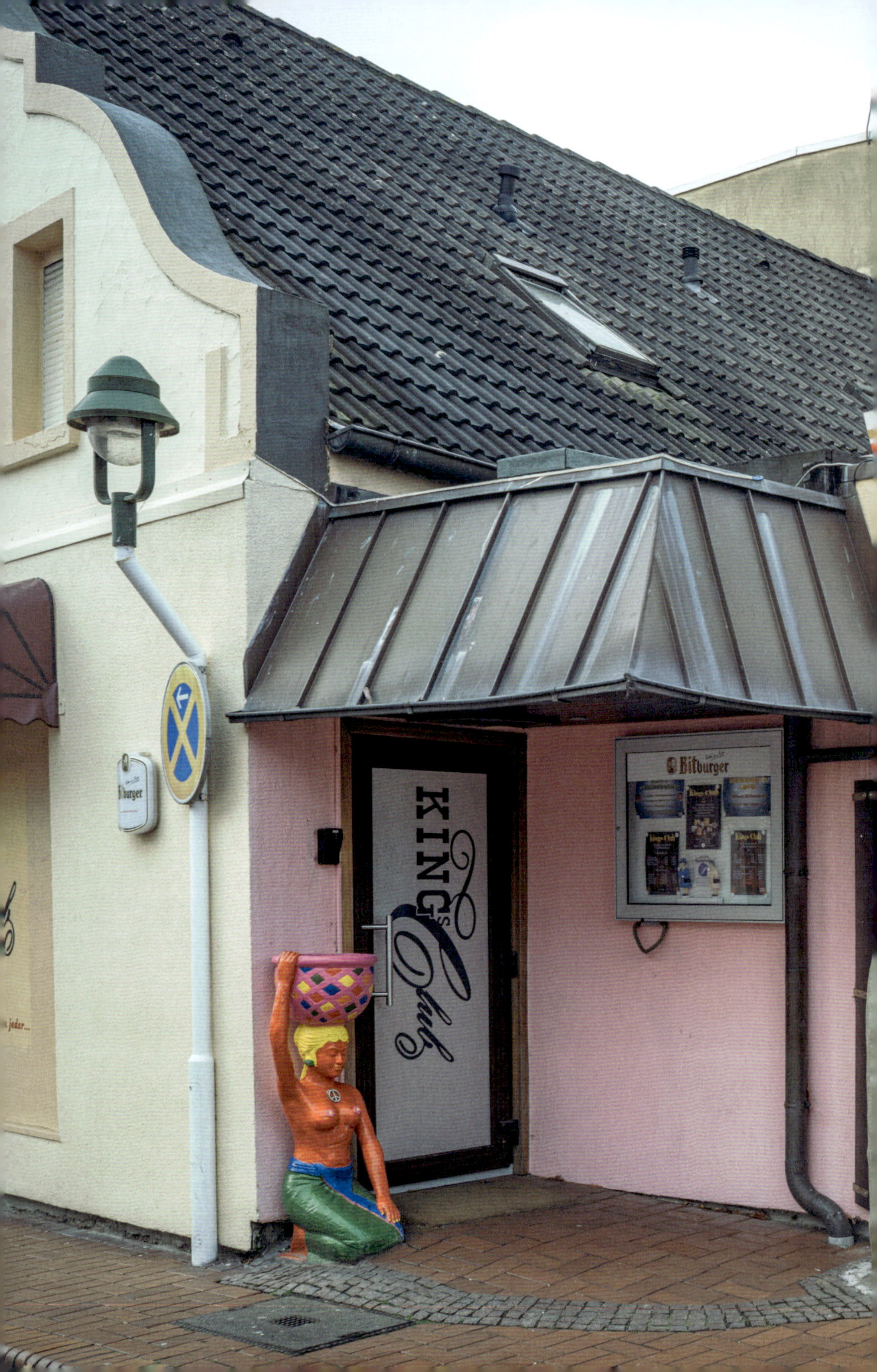
Bitburger
KING's Club
Bitburger

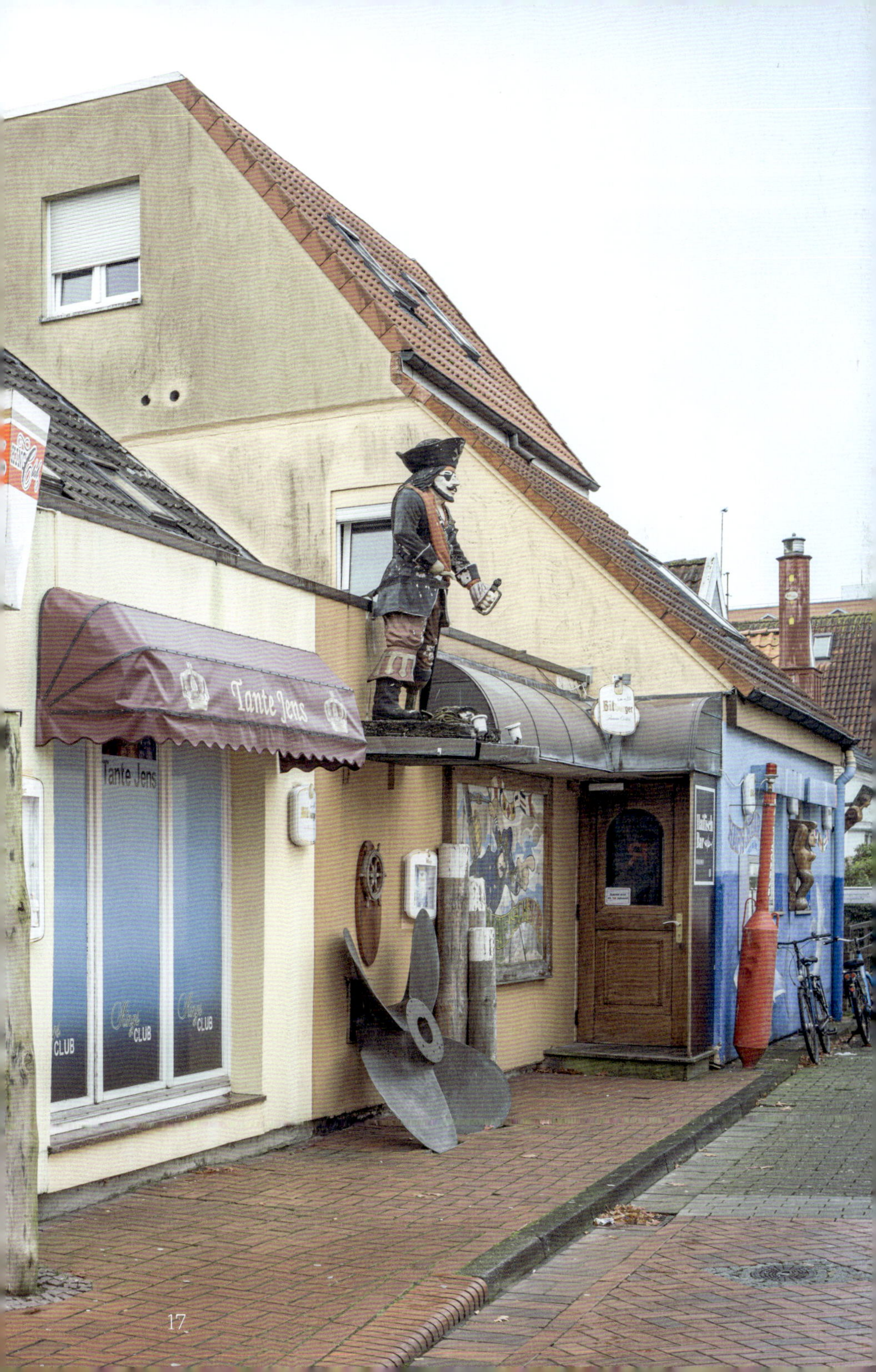
Tante Jens
Tante Jens
CLUB
CLUB
CLUB

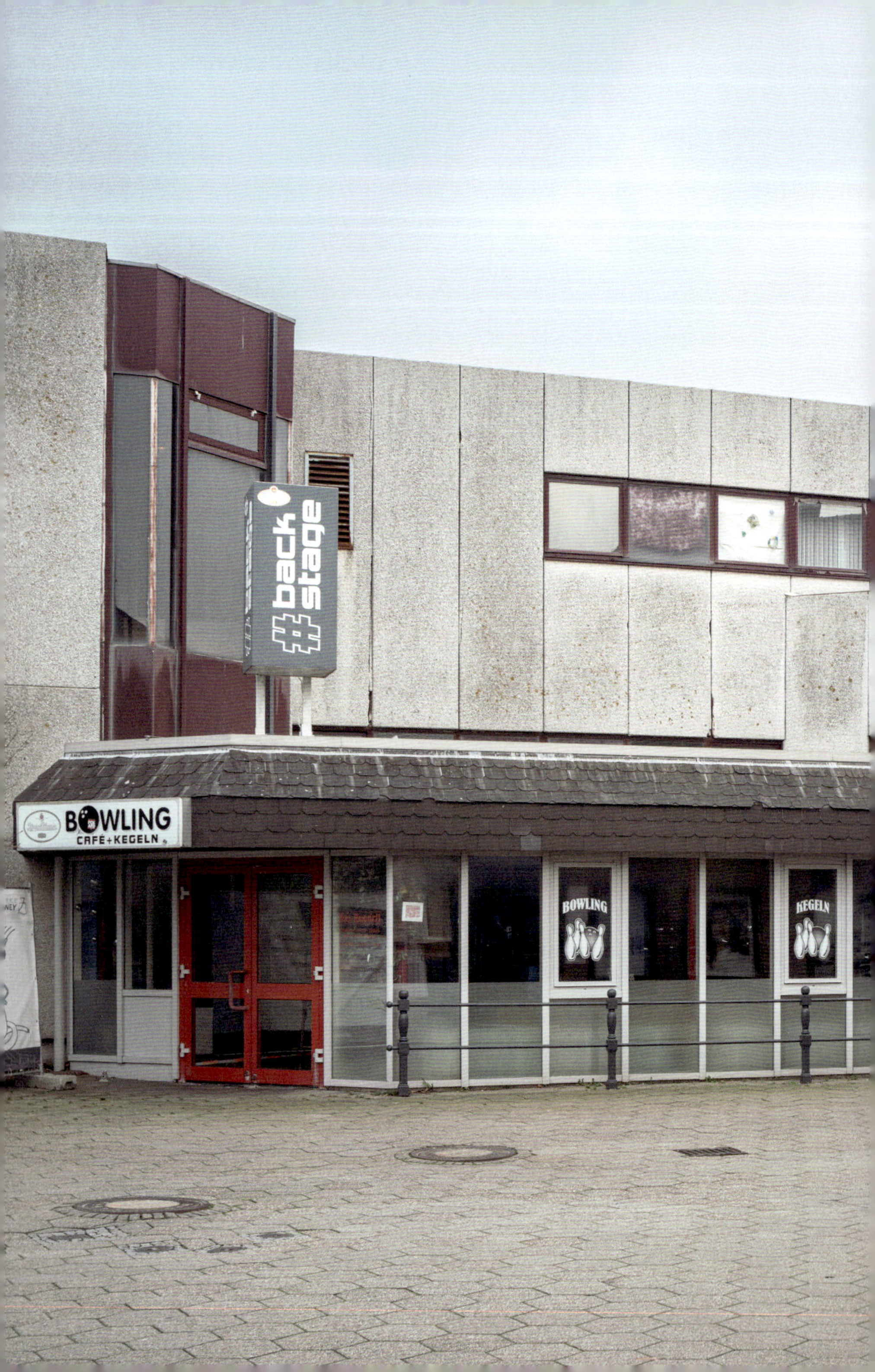

back
stage
BOWLING
CAFÉ+KEGELN
BOWLING
KEGELN

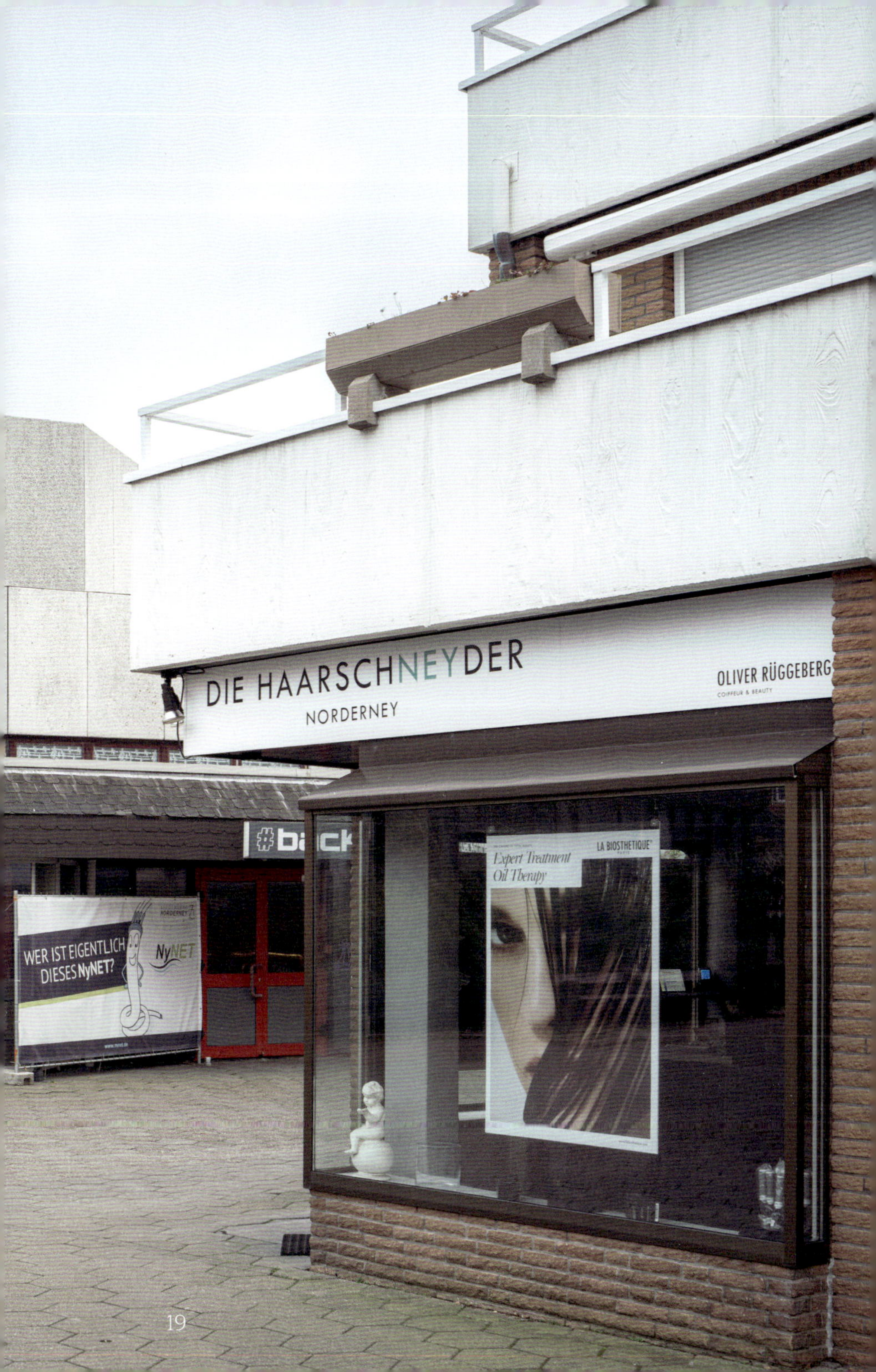
DIE HAARSCHNEYDER
NORDERNEY
OLIVER RÜGGEBERG
COIFFEUR & BEAUTY
LA BIOSTHETIQUE
Expert Treatment
Oil Therapy
WER IST EIGENTLICH
DIESES NyNET?
NyNET

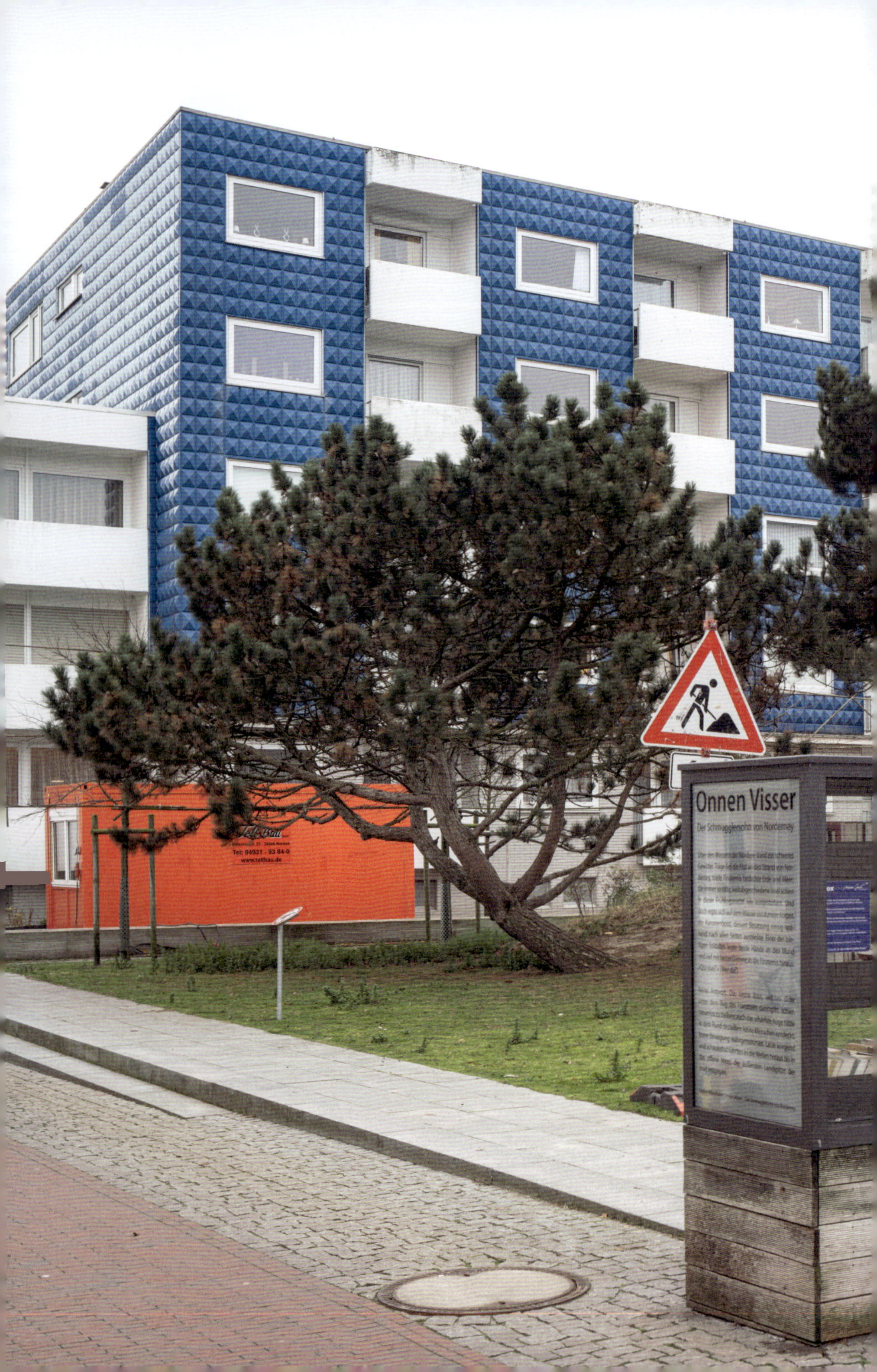
Onnen Visser
Der Schmugglersohn von Norderney

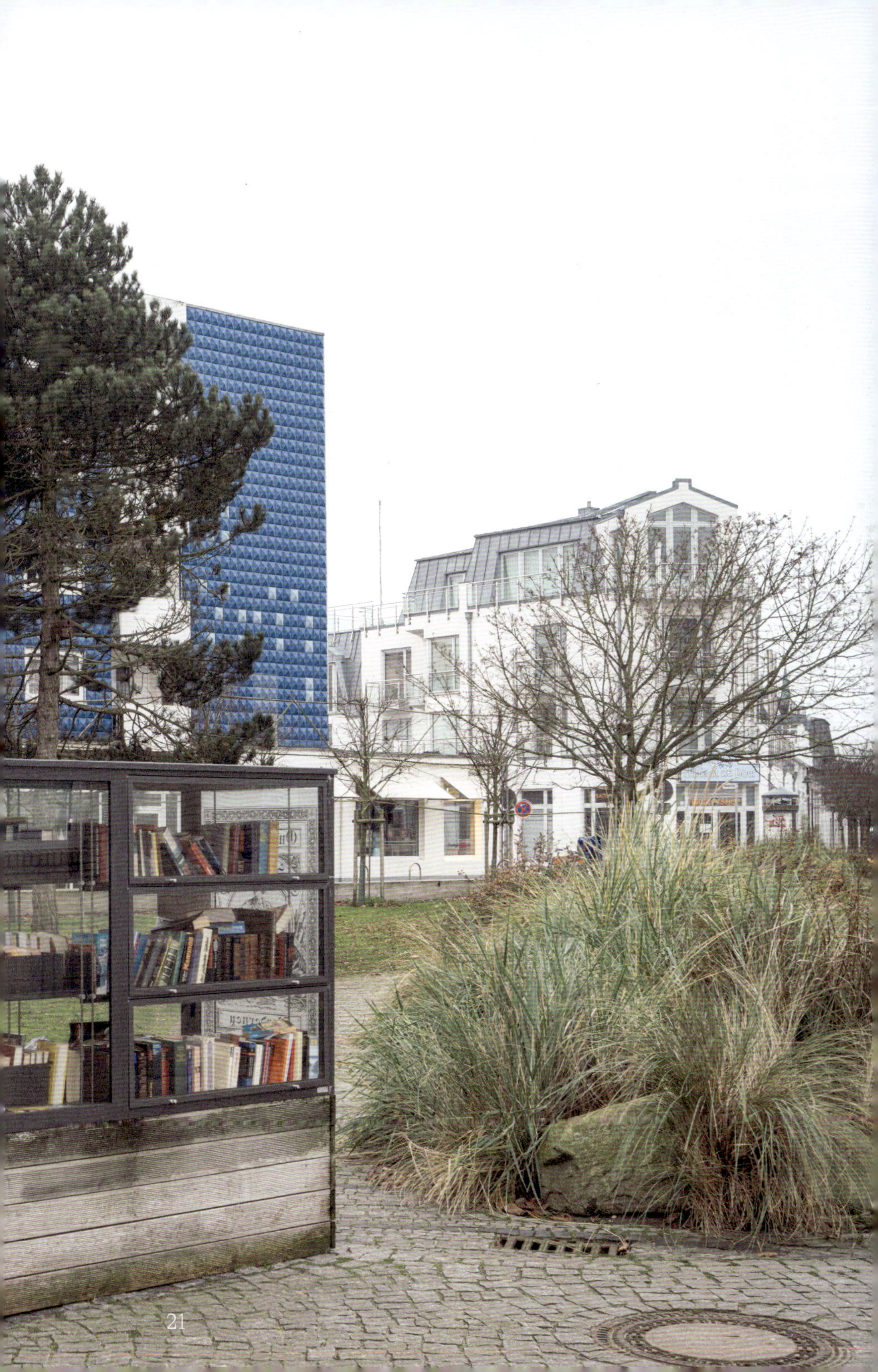

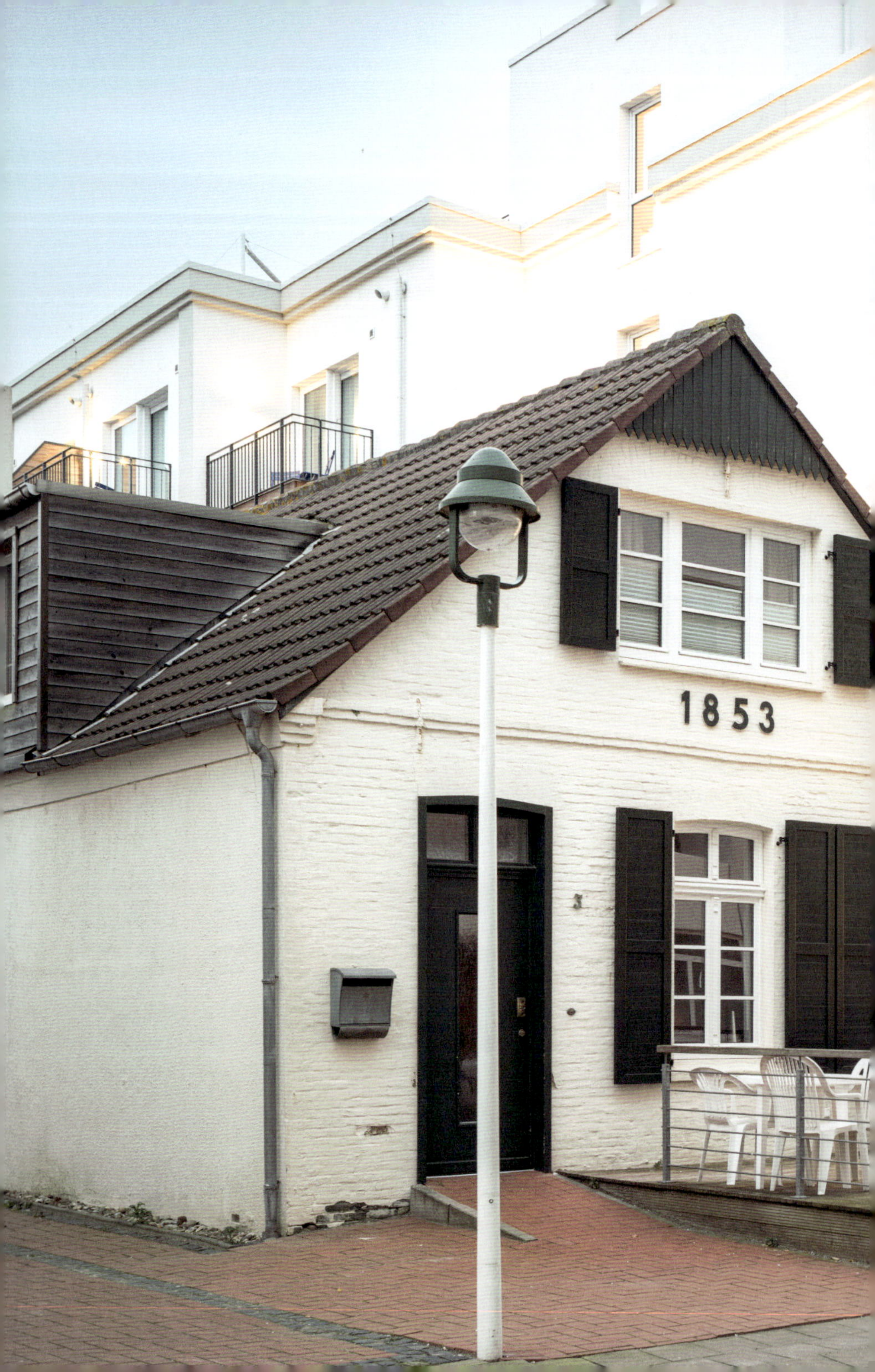
1853

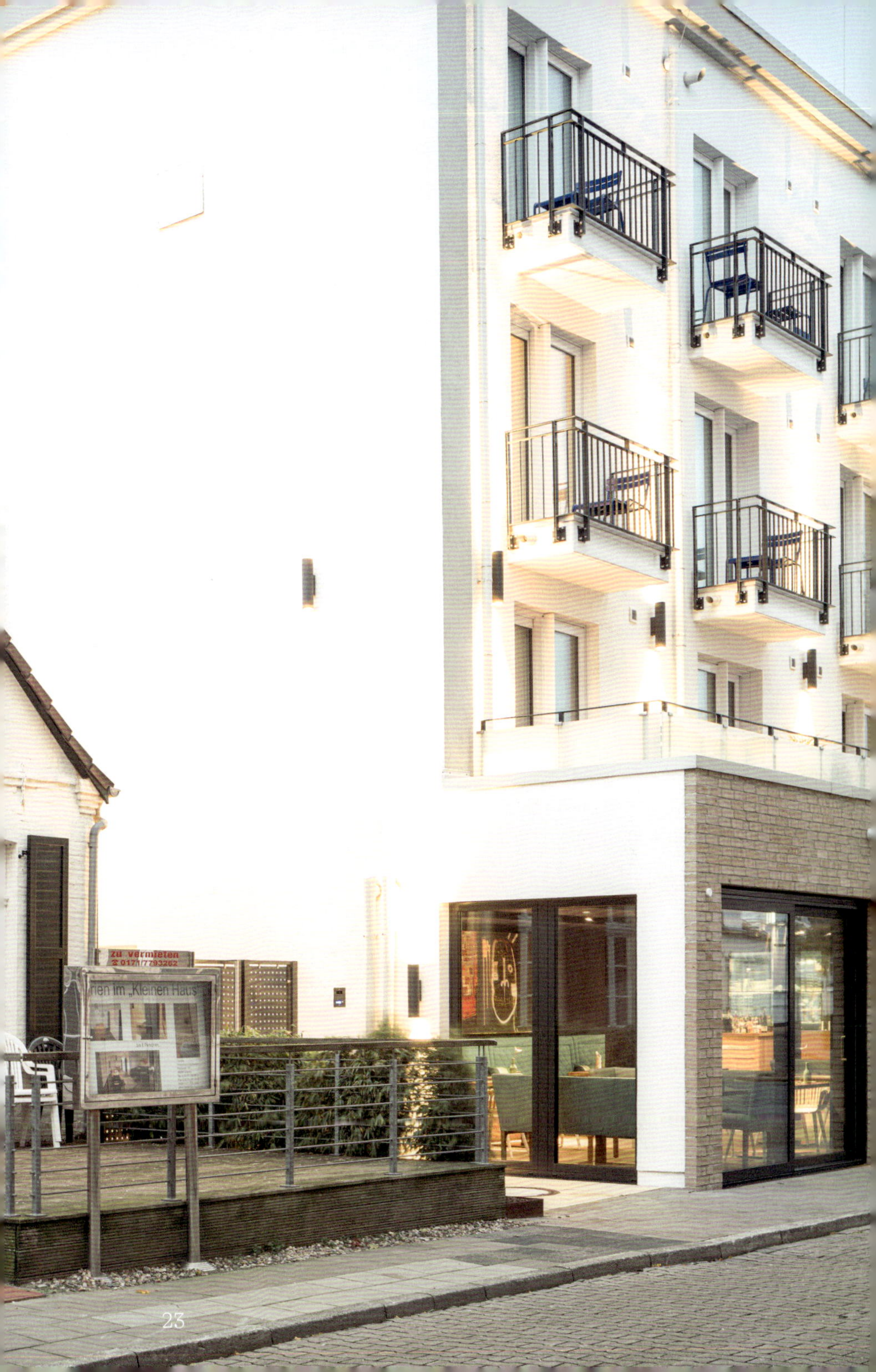
zu vermieten
0171/7793262
rien im „Kleinen Haus

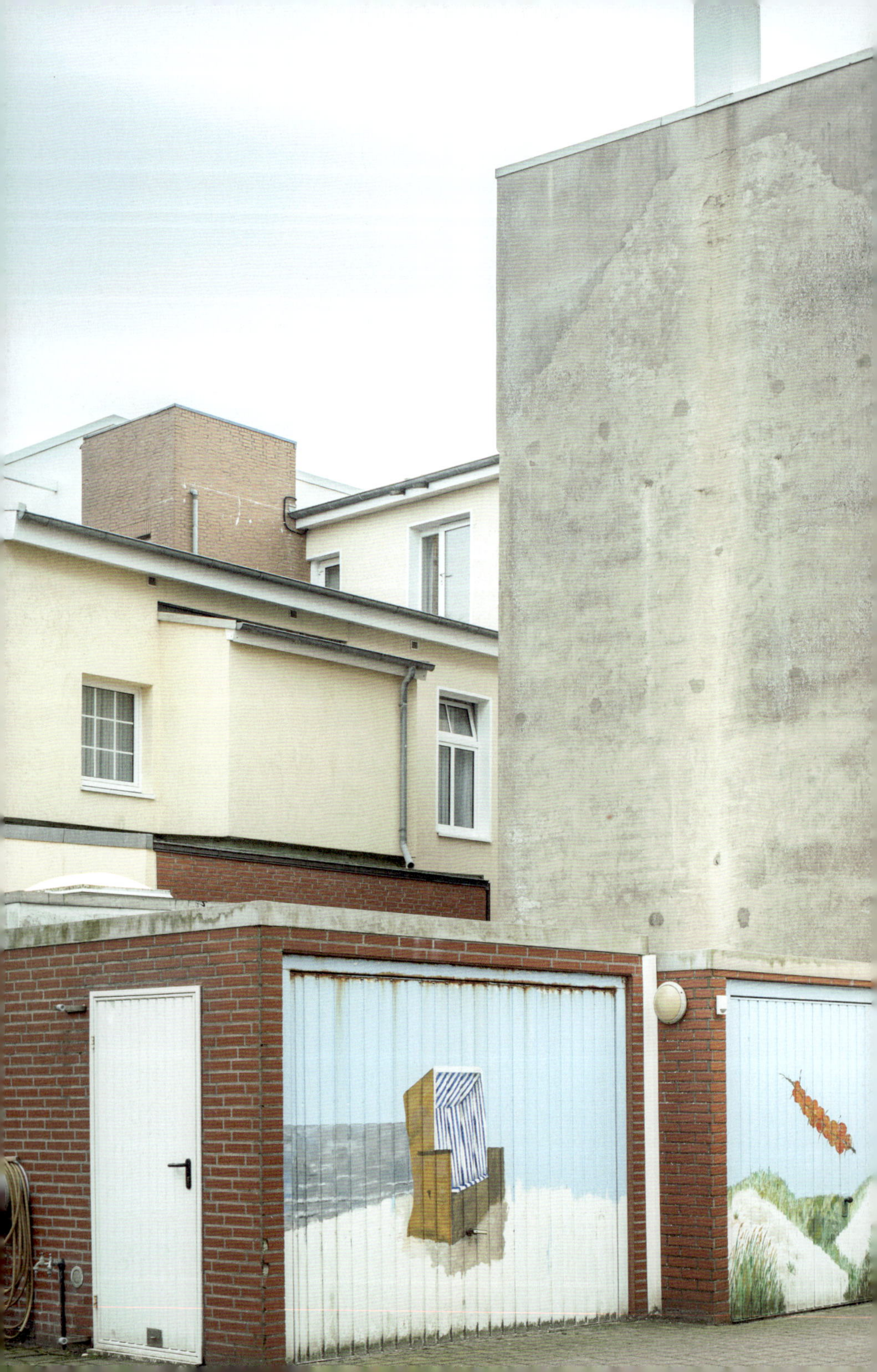

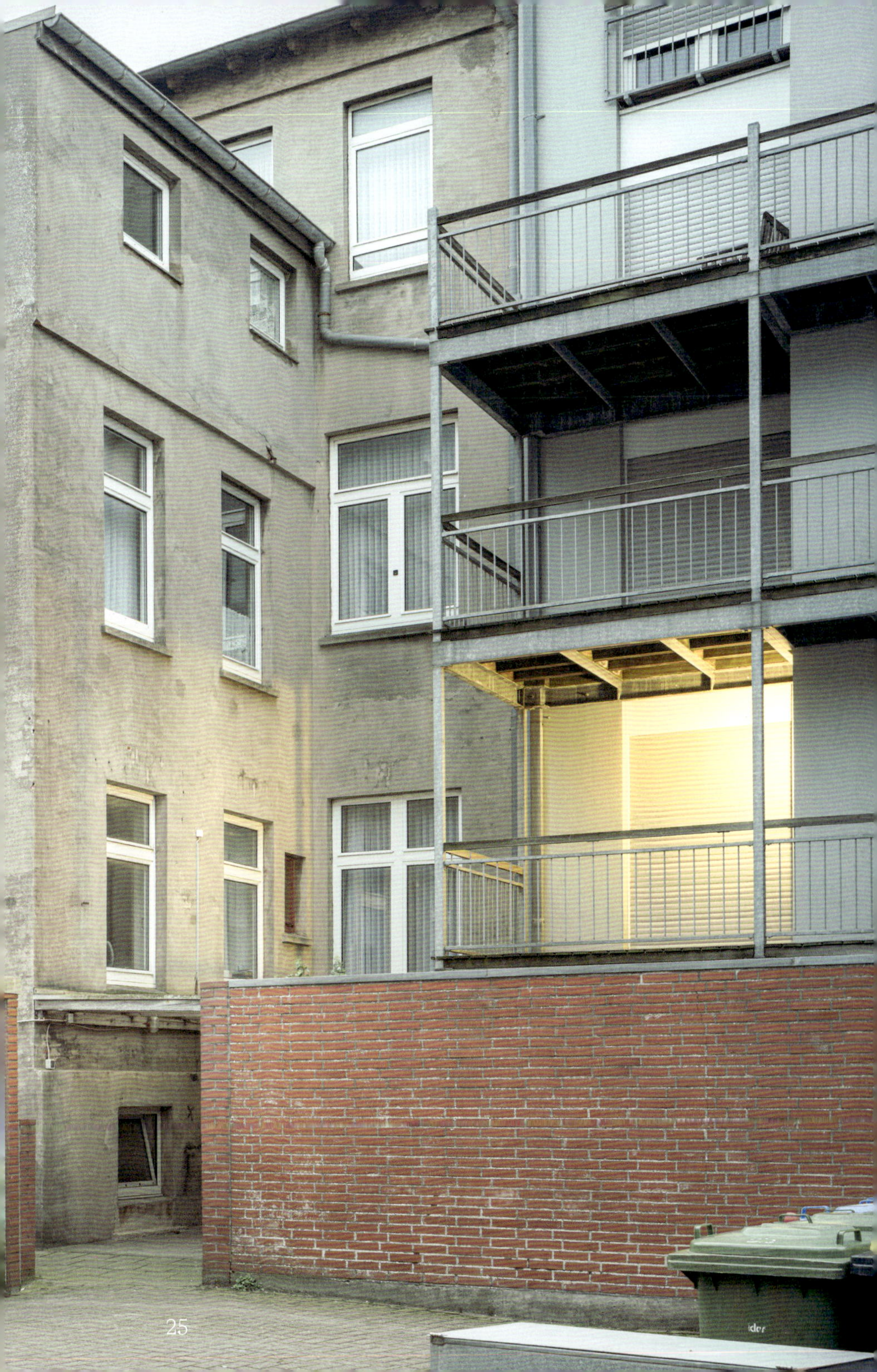

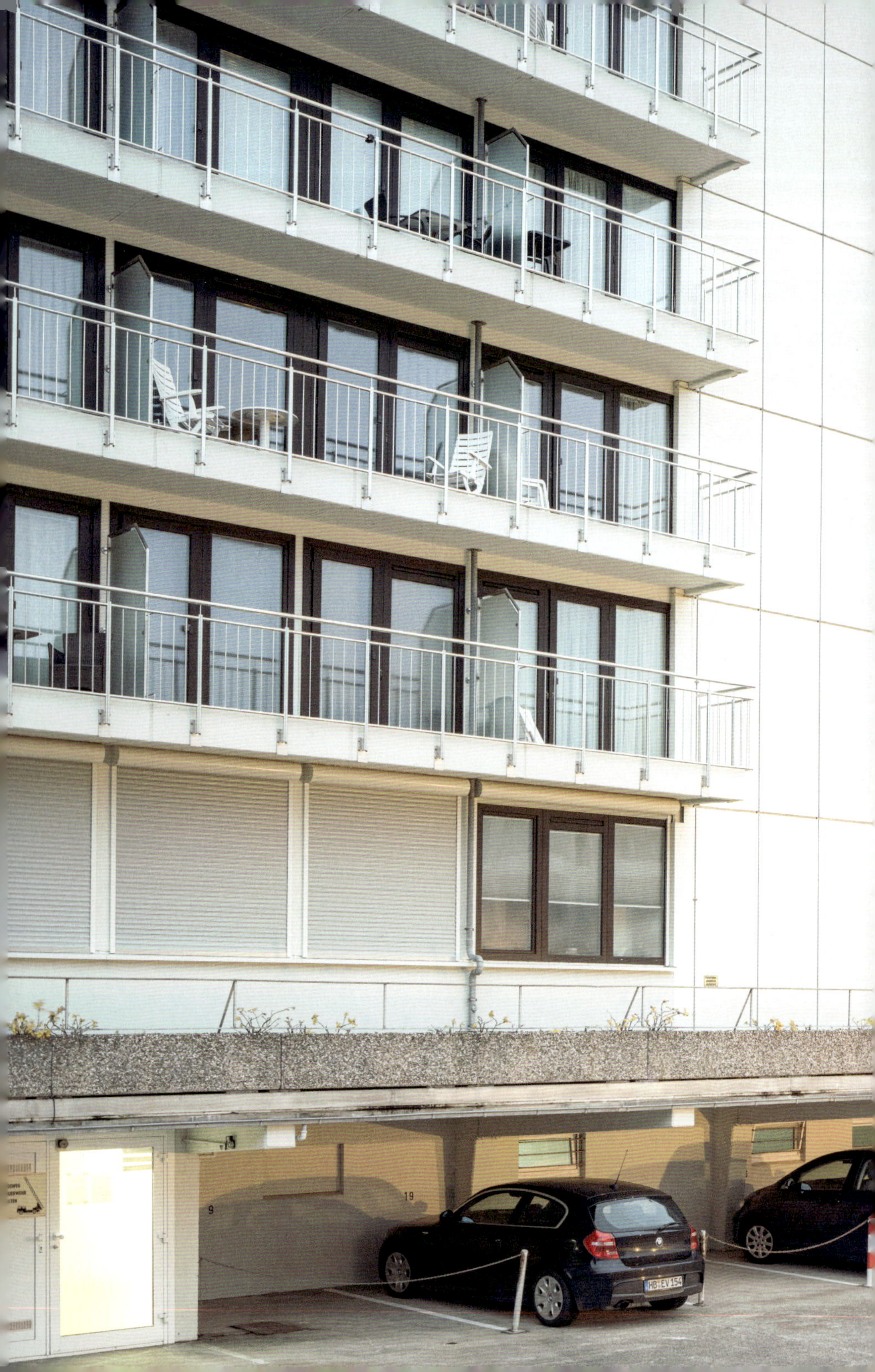
9
19
HB EV 154

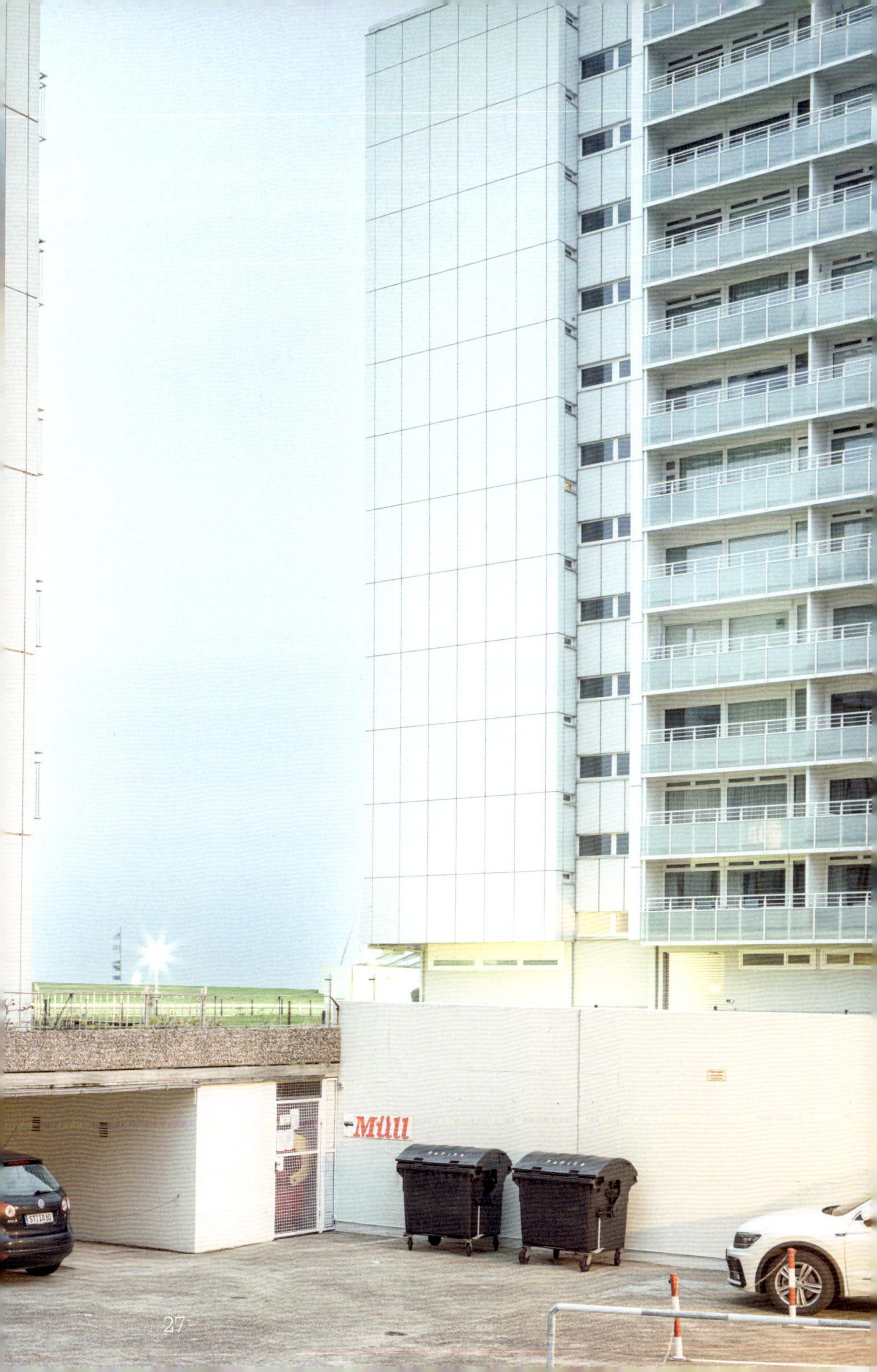
Müll

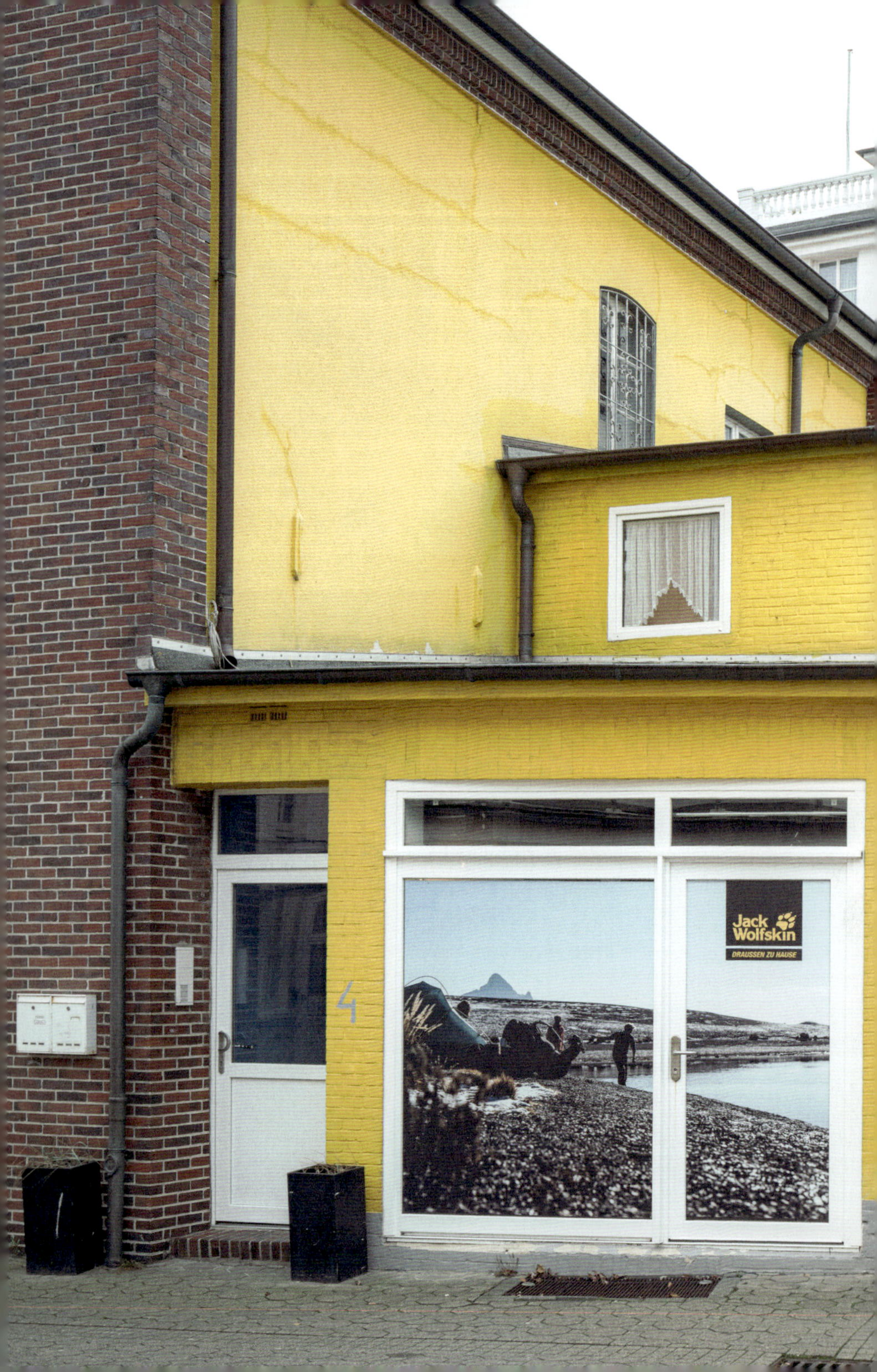
Jack
Wolfskin
DRAUSSEN ZU HAUSE
4

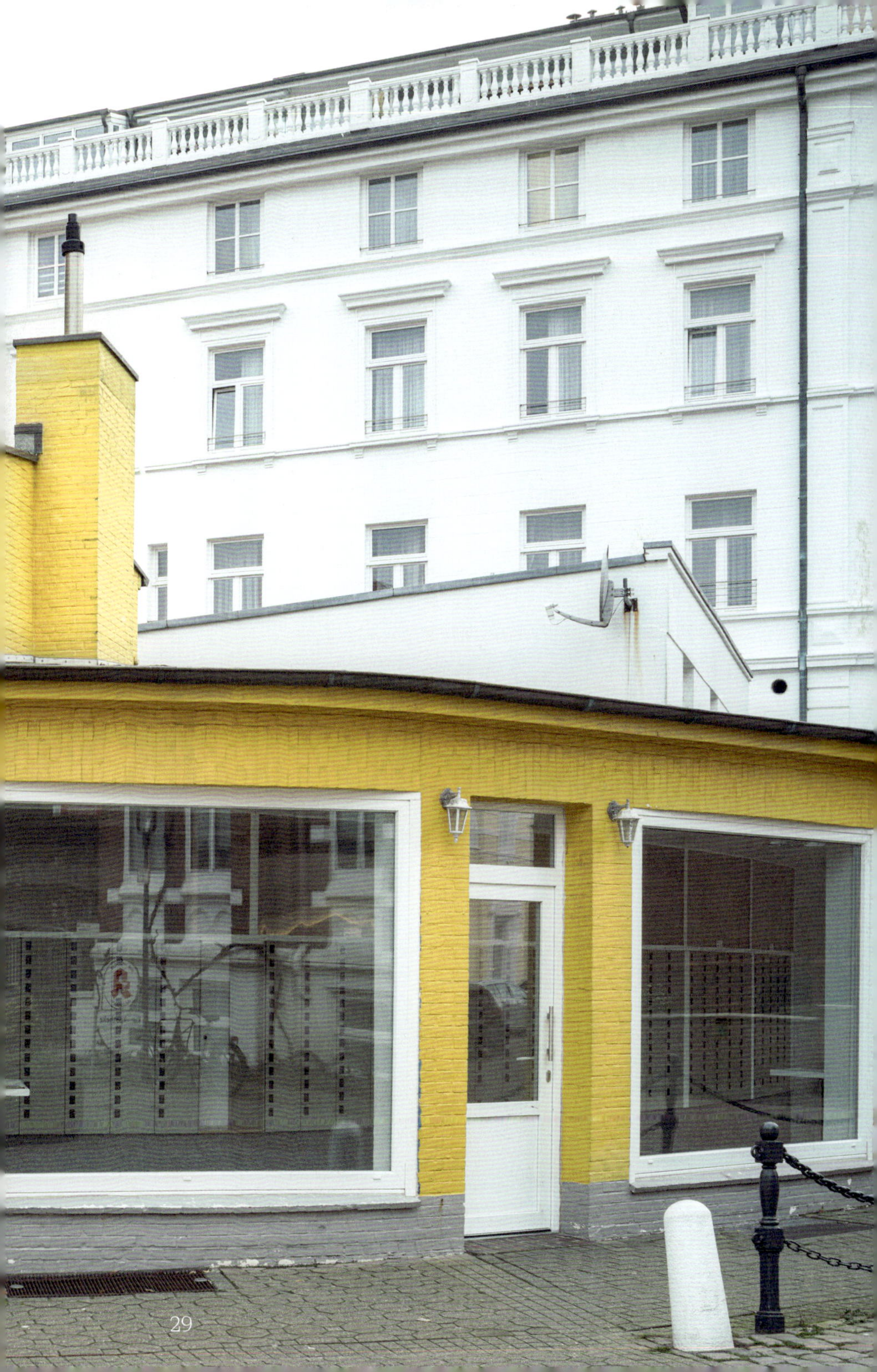

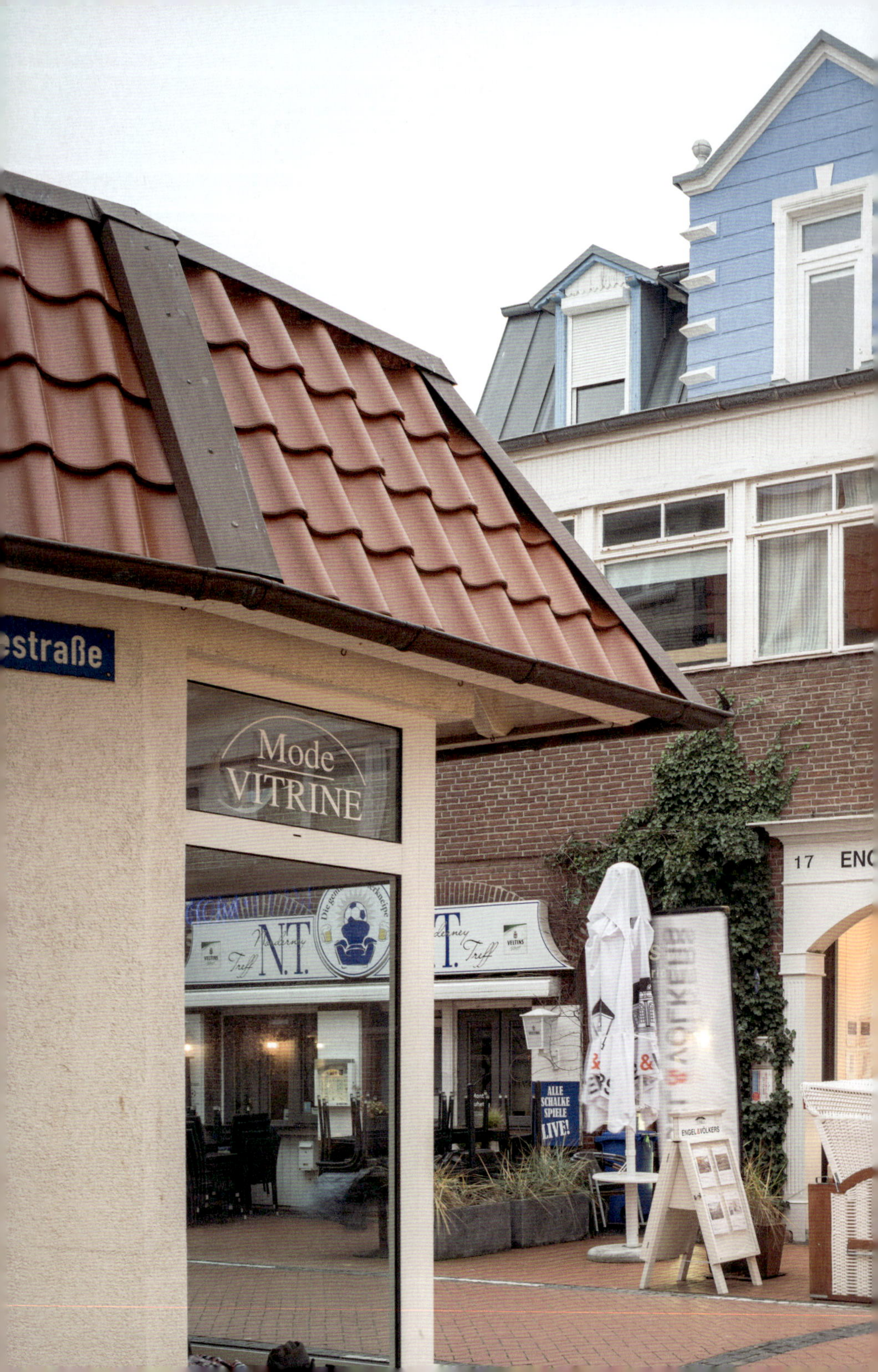
estraße
Mode
VITRINE
N.T.
ALLE
SCHALKE
SPIELE
LIVE!
ENGEL & VÖLKERS
17

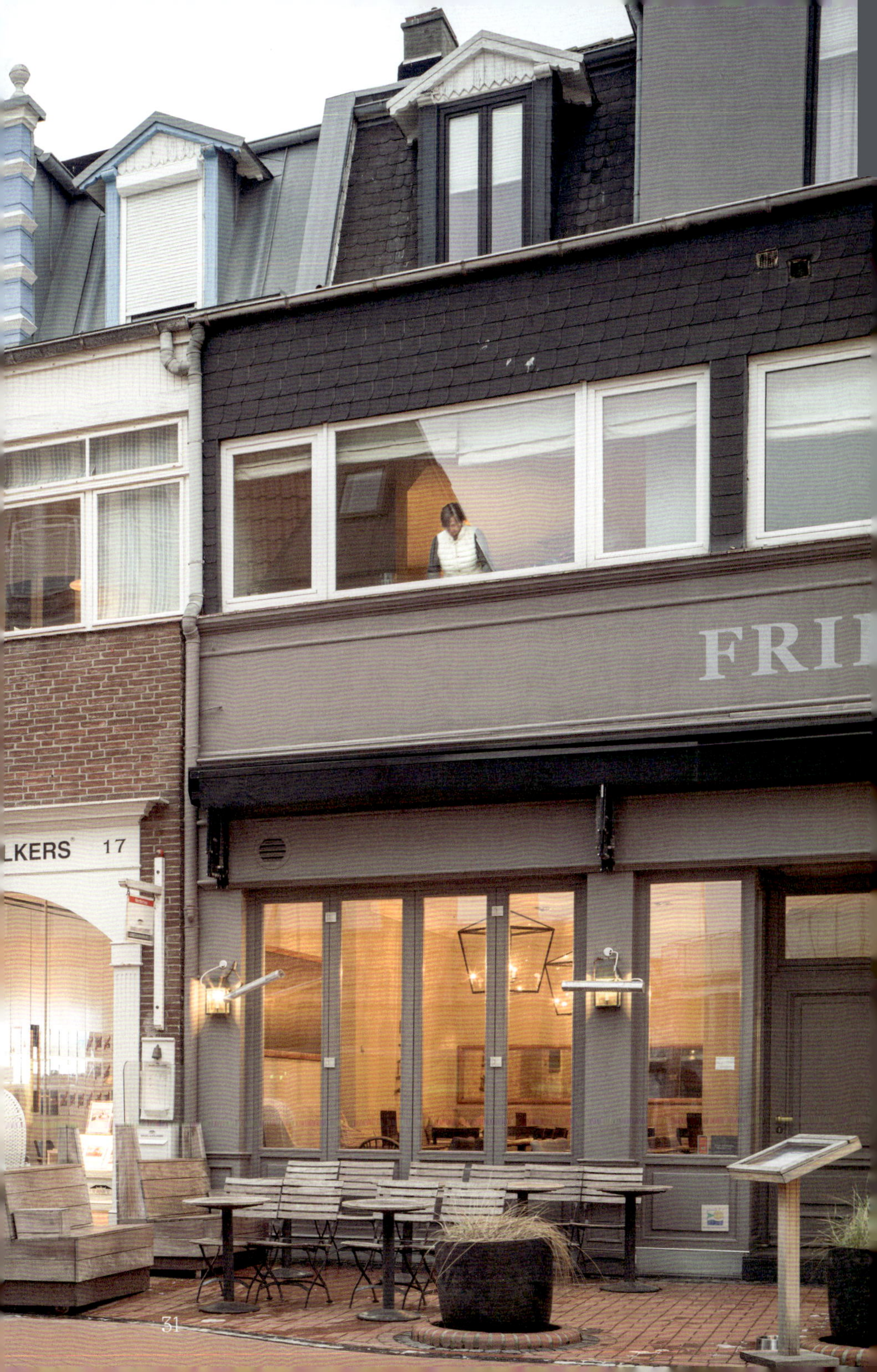
FRI
LKERS
17

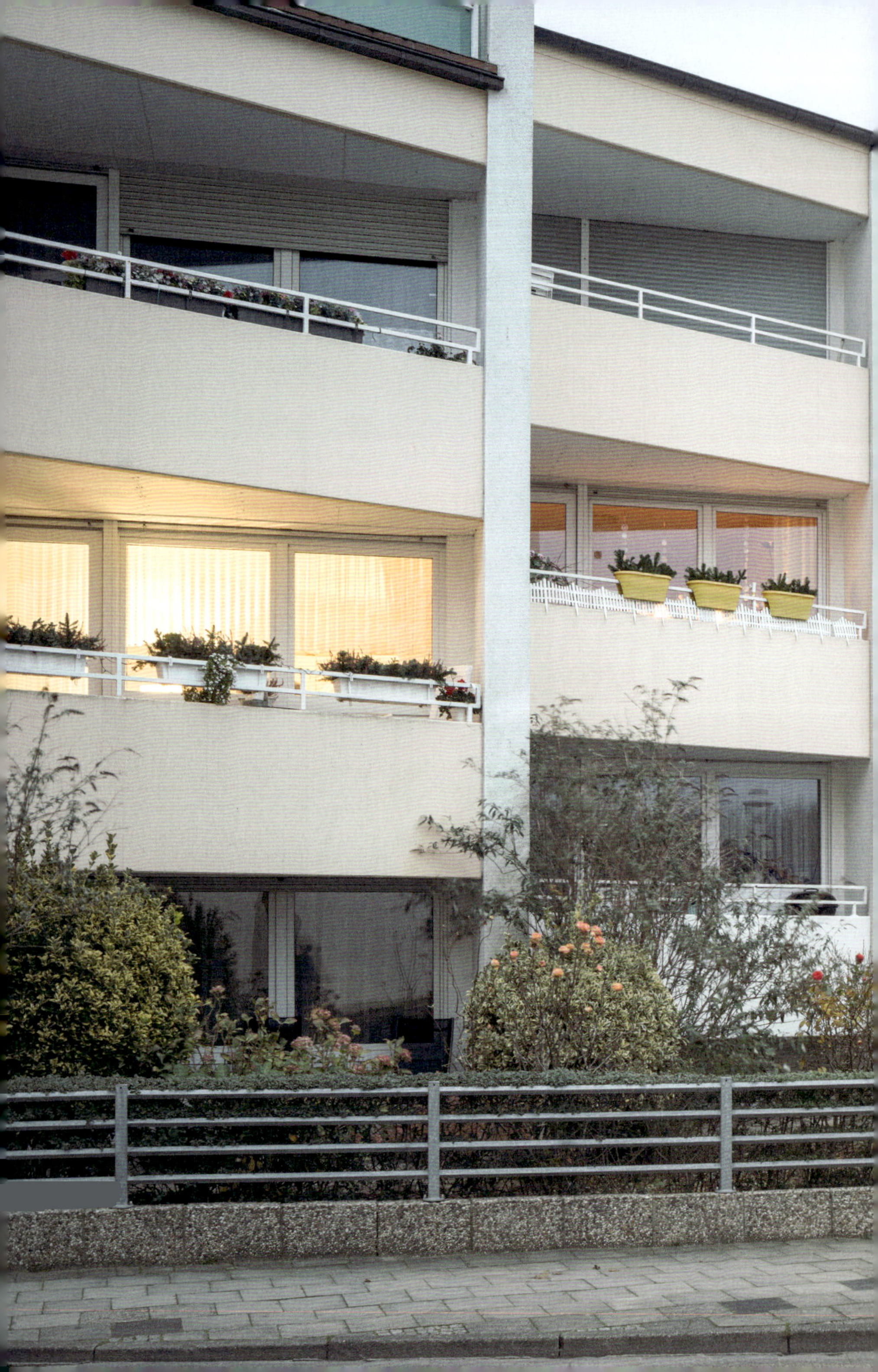

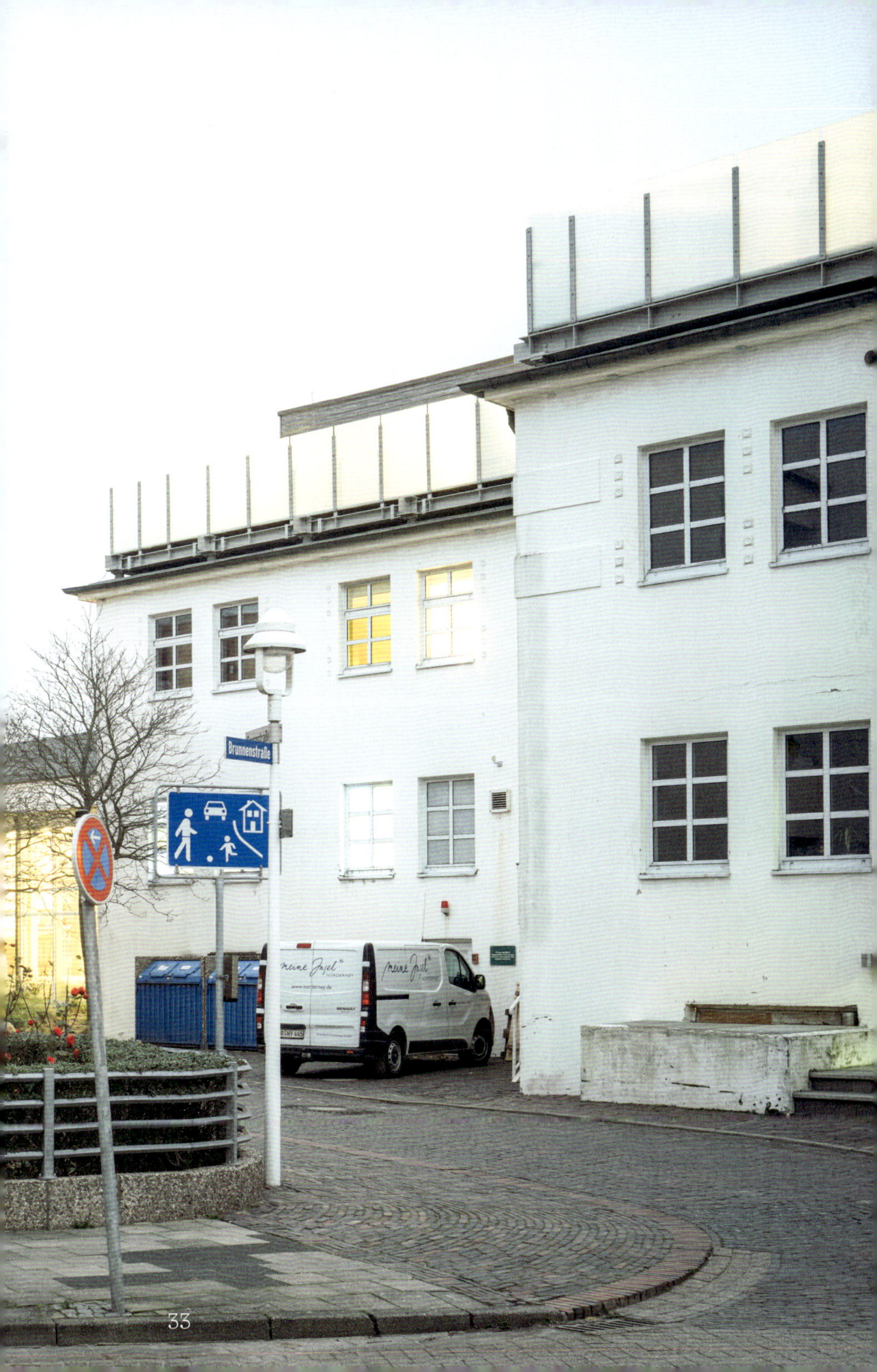
Brunnenstraße
www.norderney.de

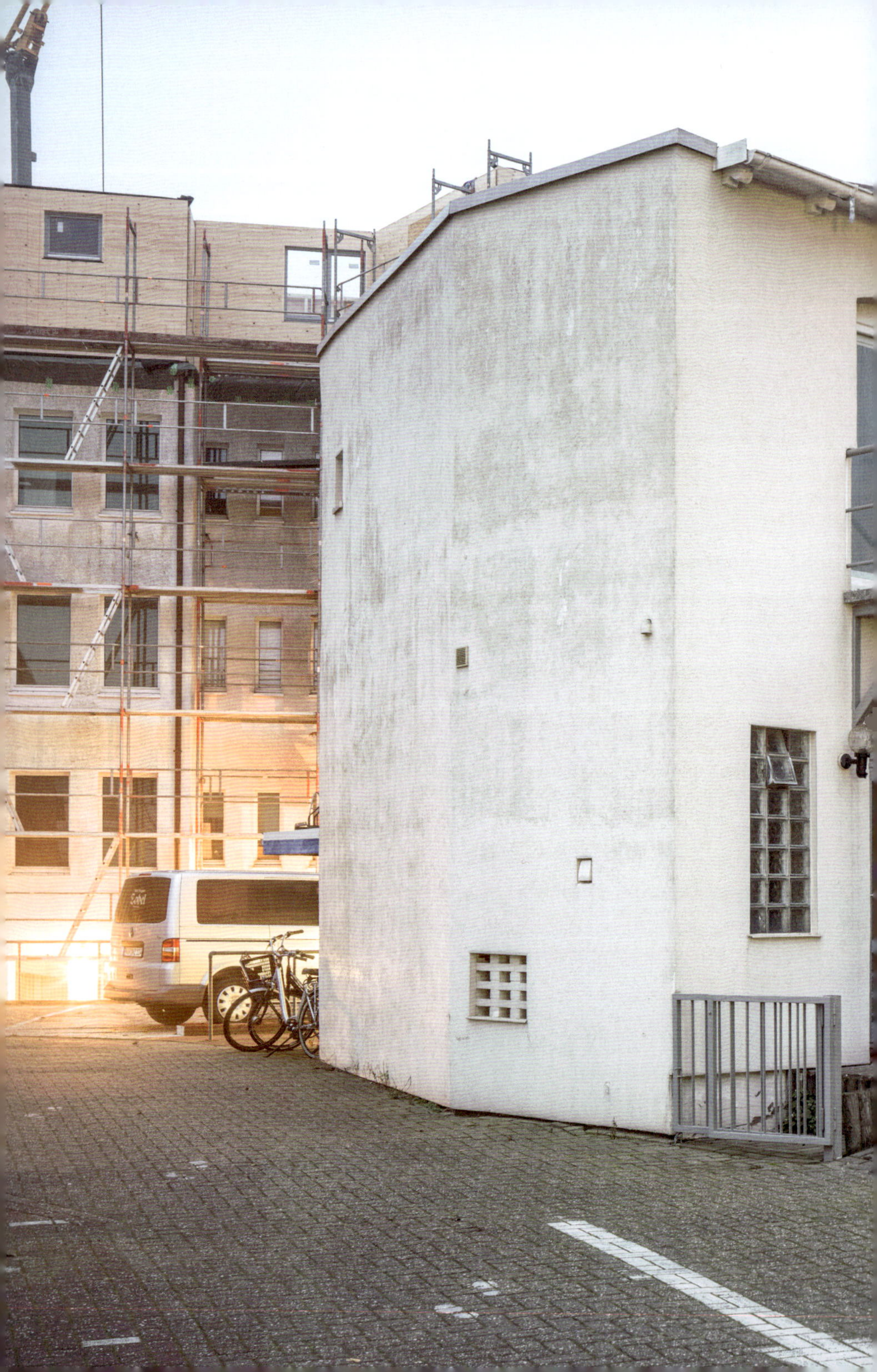

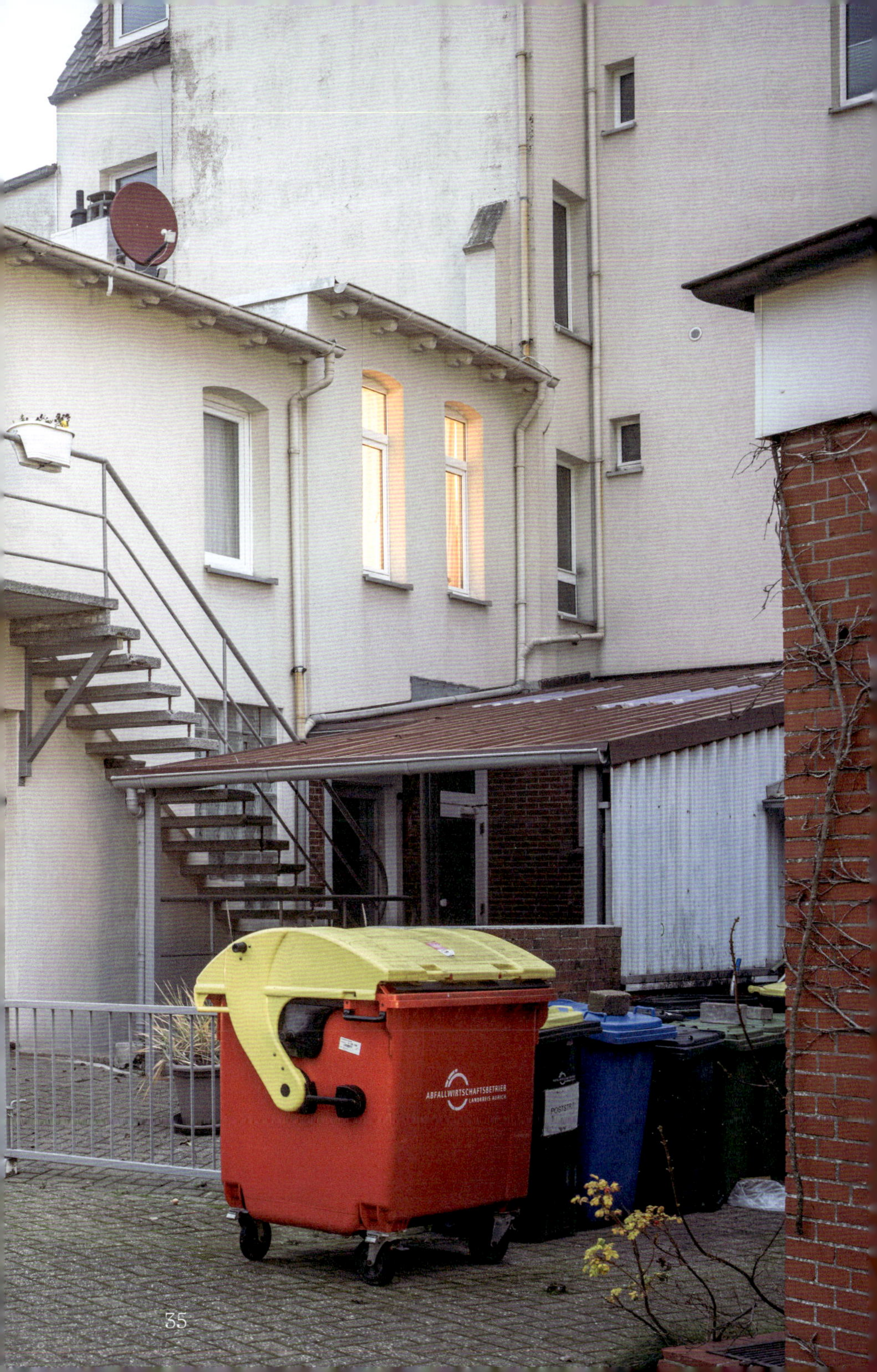
ABFALLWIRTSCHAFTSBETRIEB
LANDKREIS AURICH

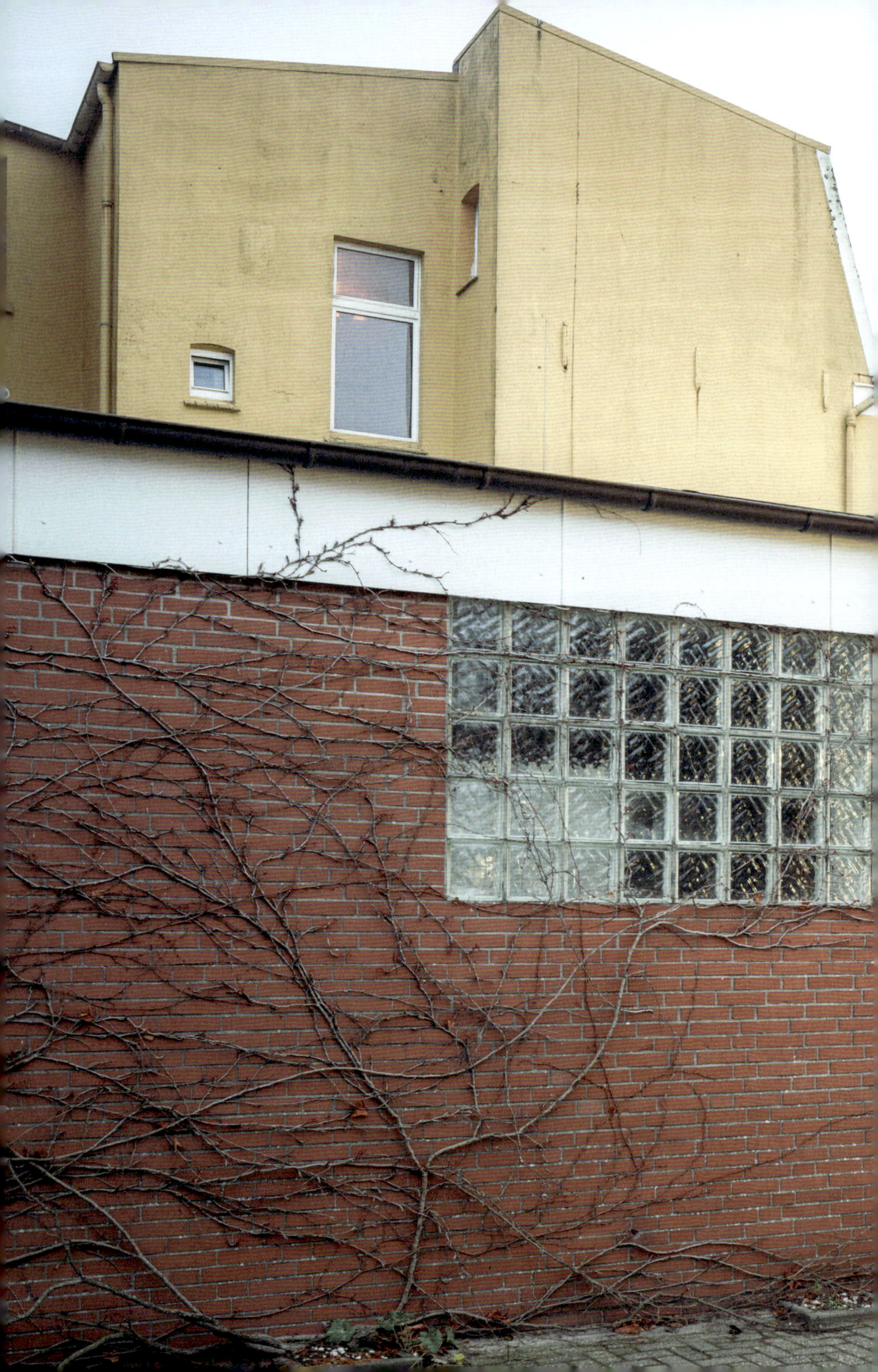

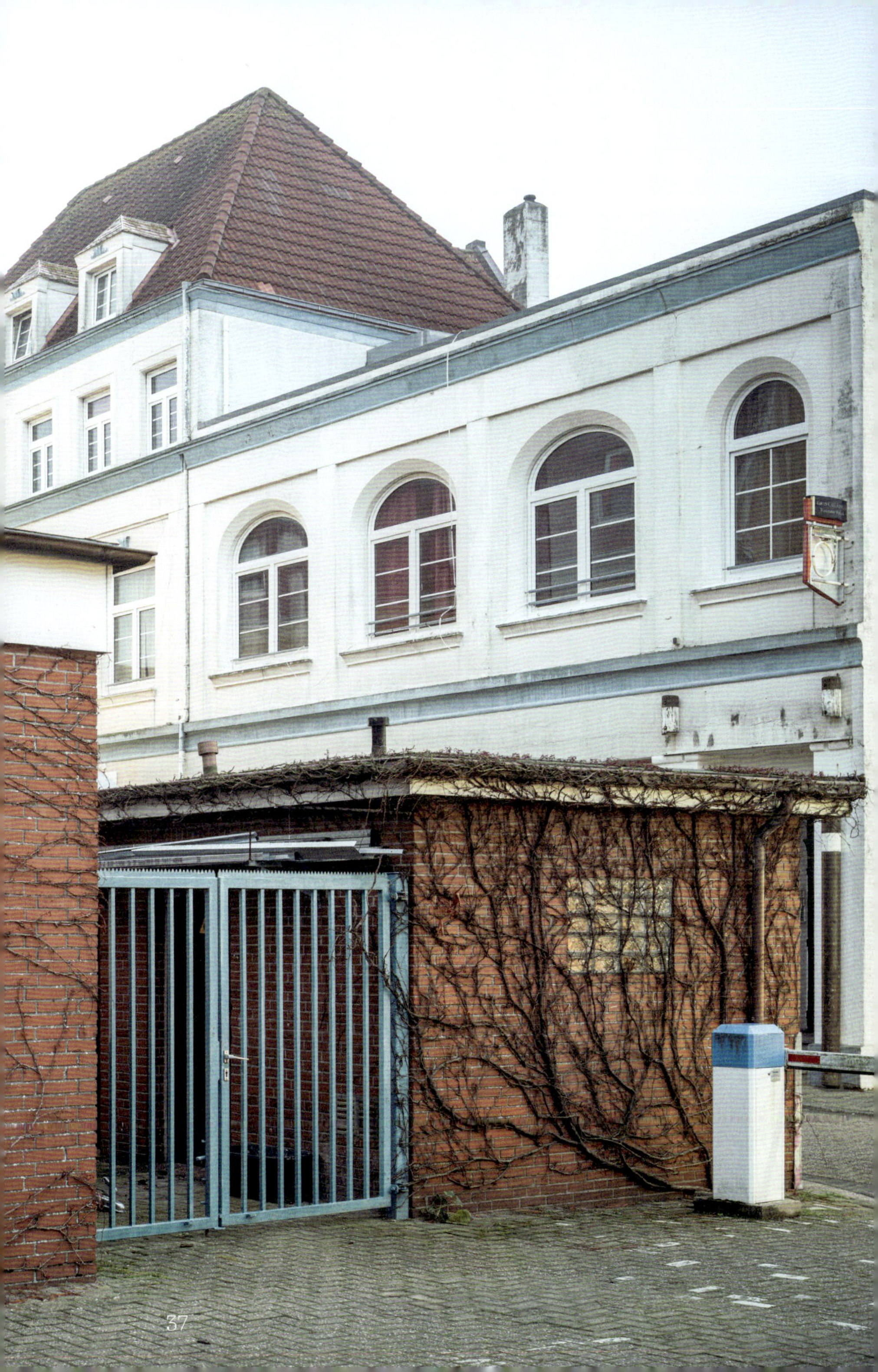

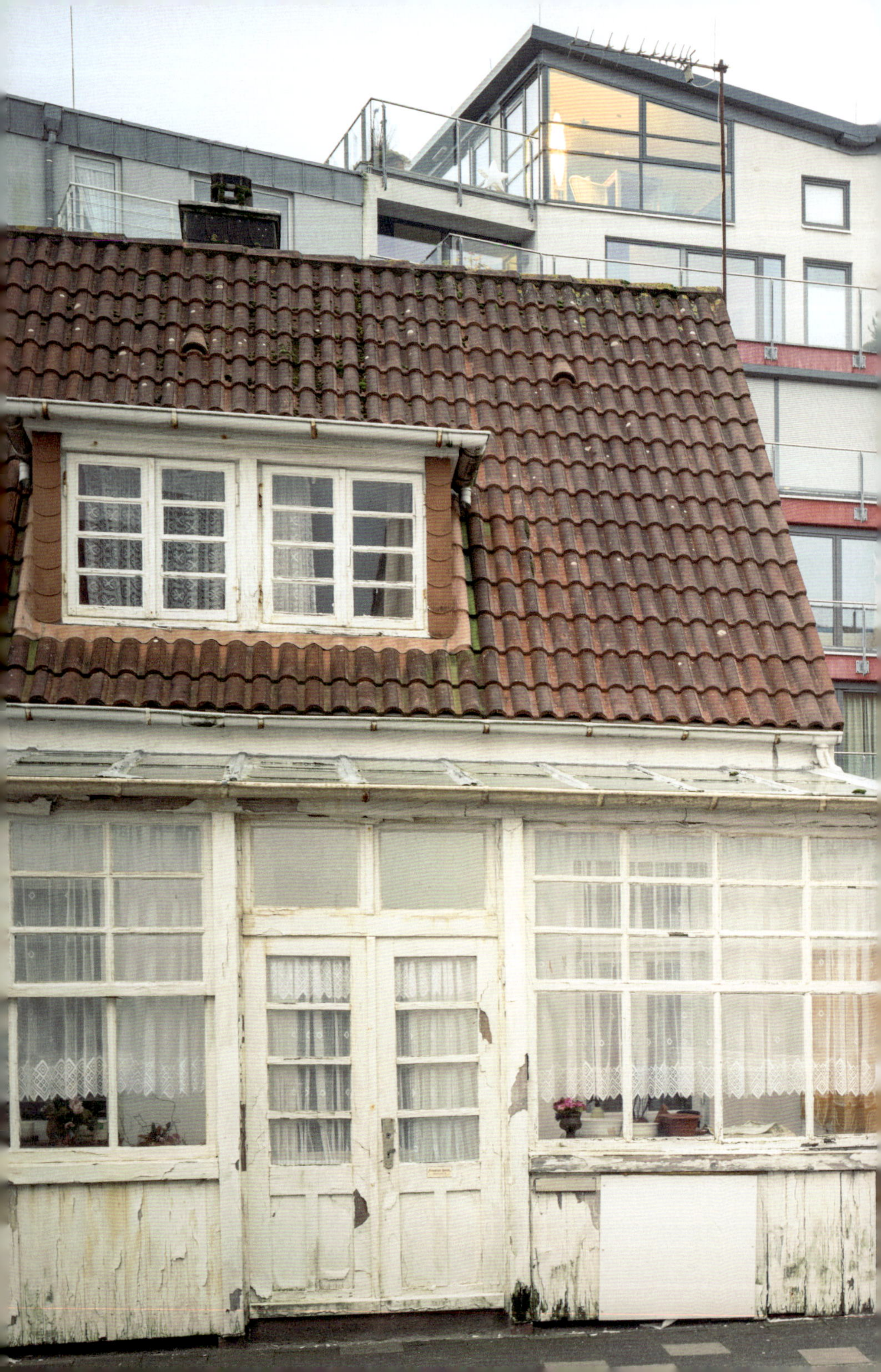

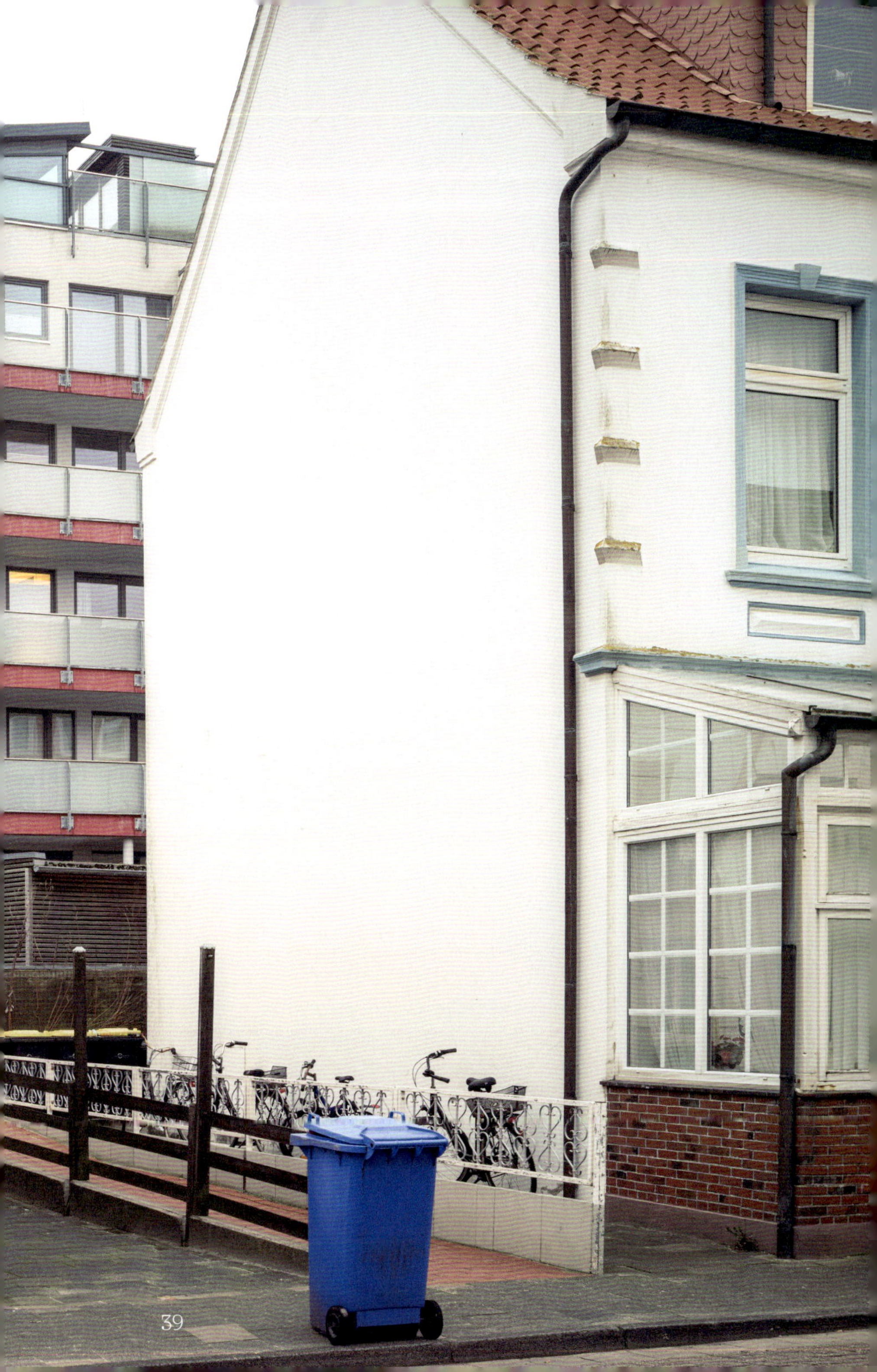

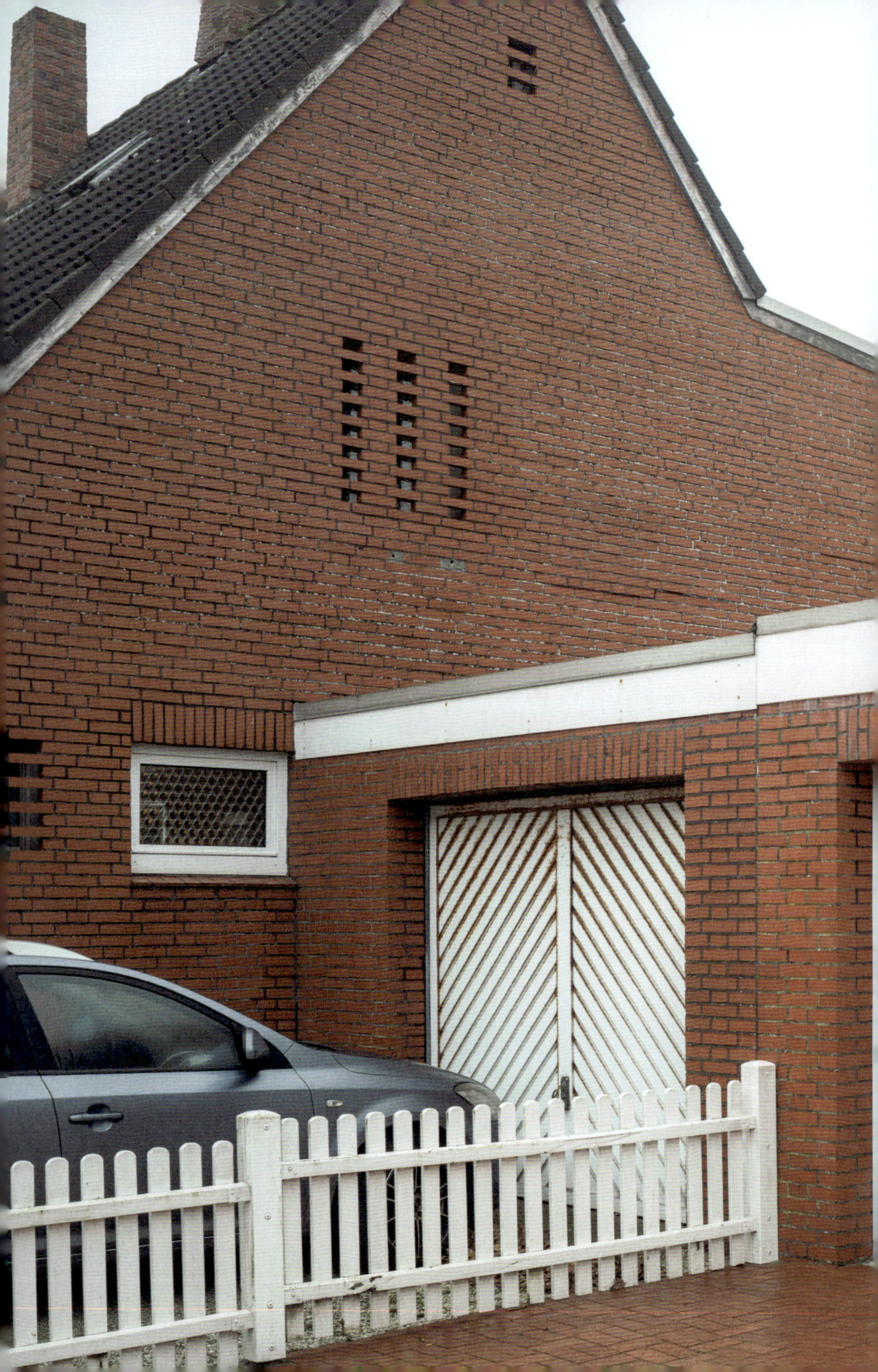

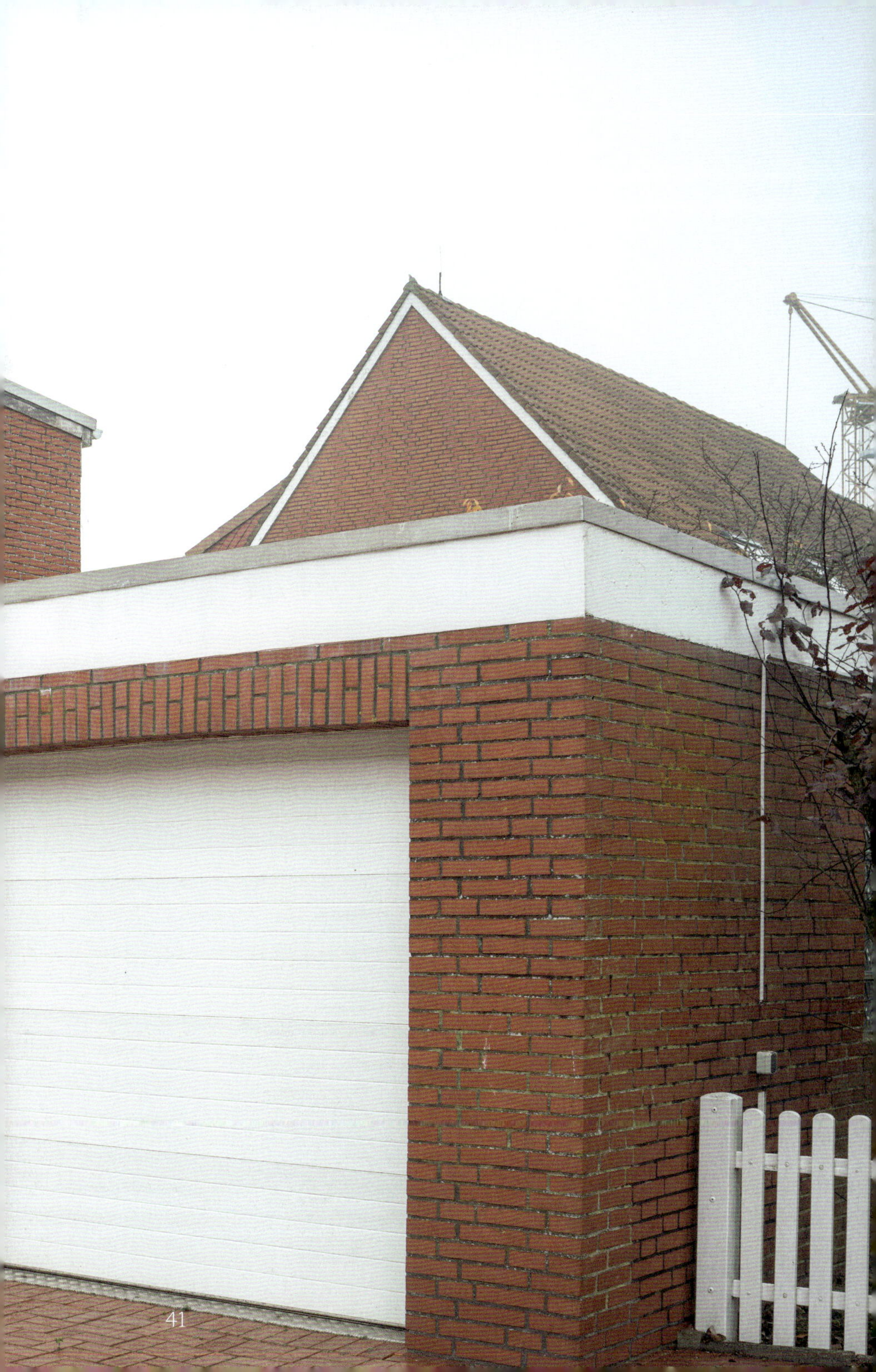

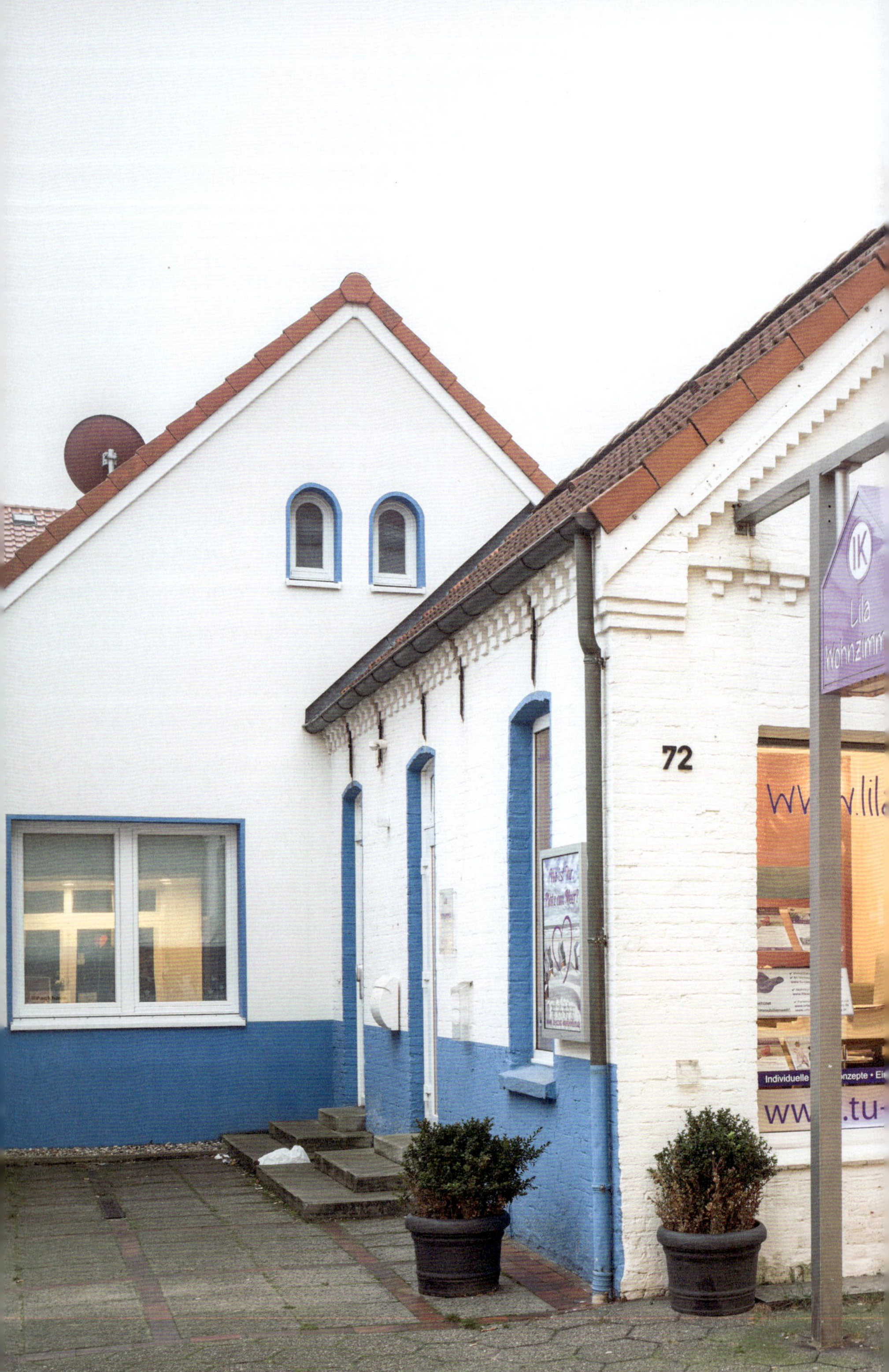
IK
Lila
72
Individuelle

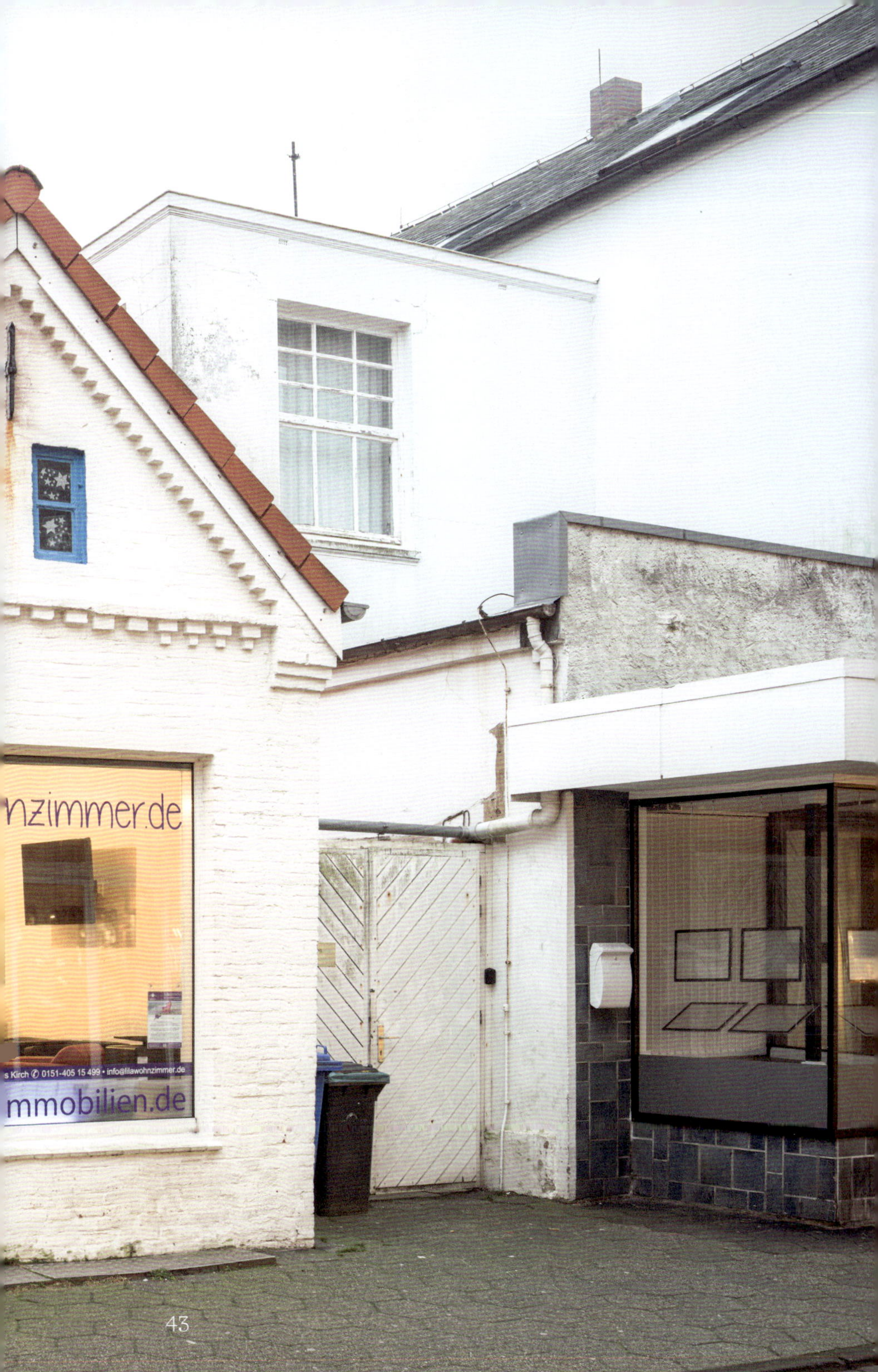
nzimmer.de
s Kirch ✆ 0151-405 15 499 • info@lilawohnzimmer.de
mmobilien.de

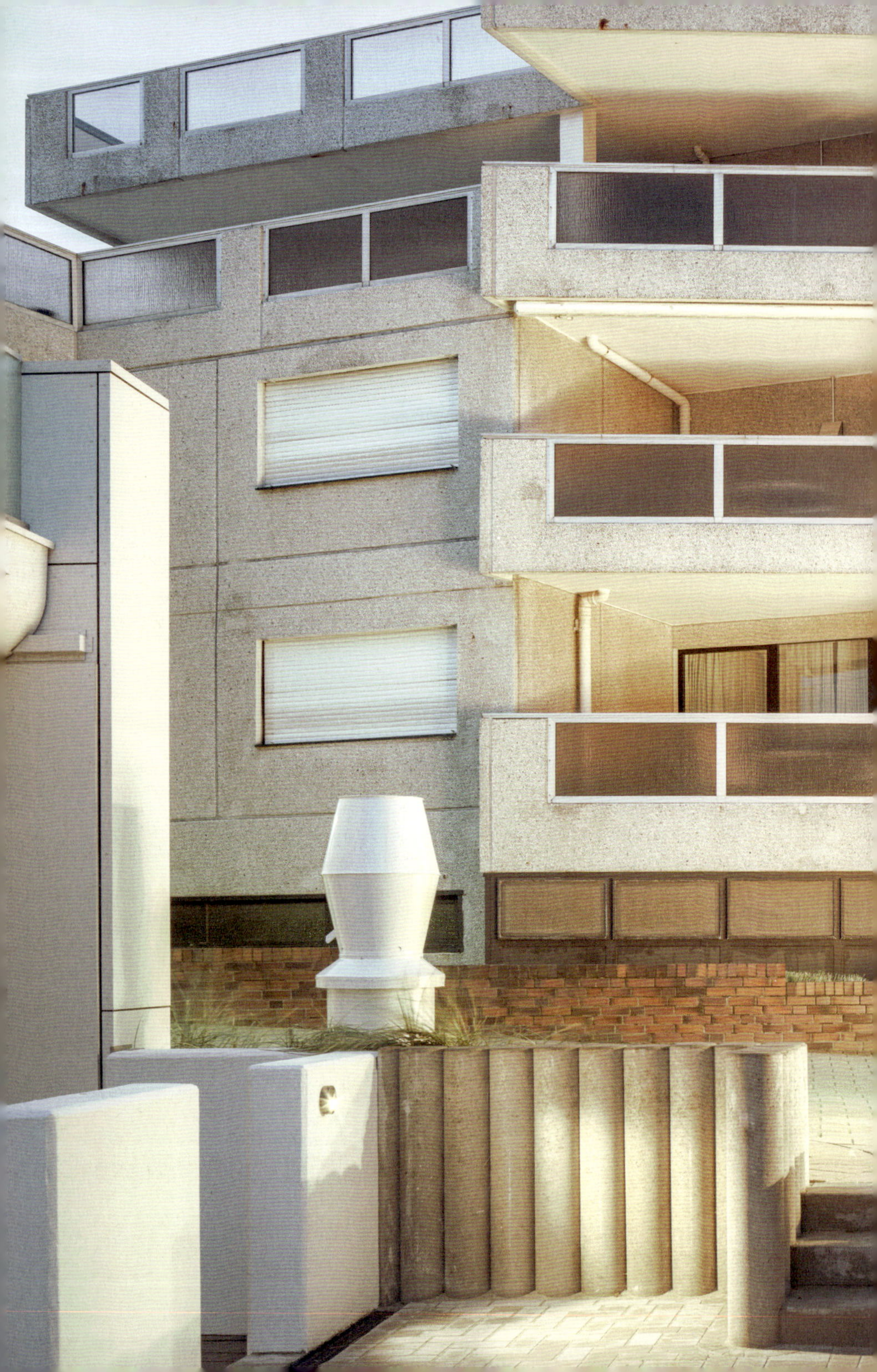

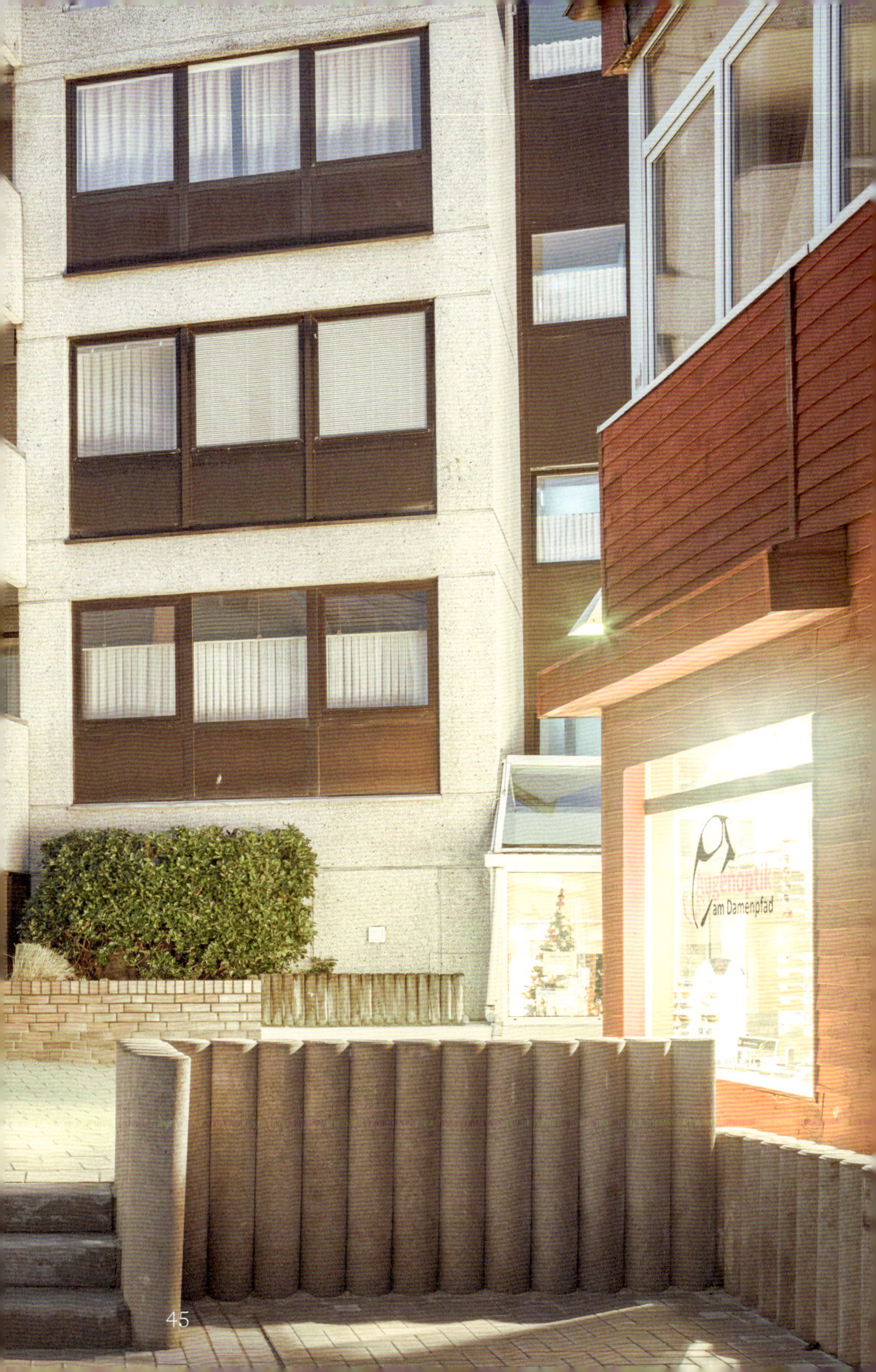
Augenoptik
am Damenpfad

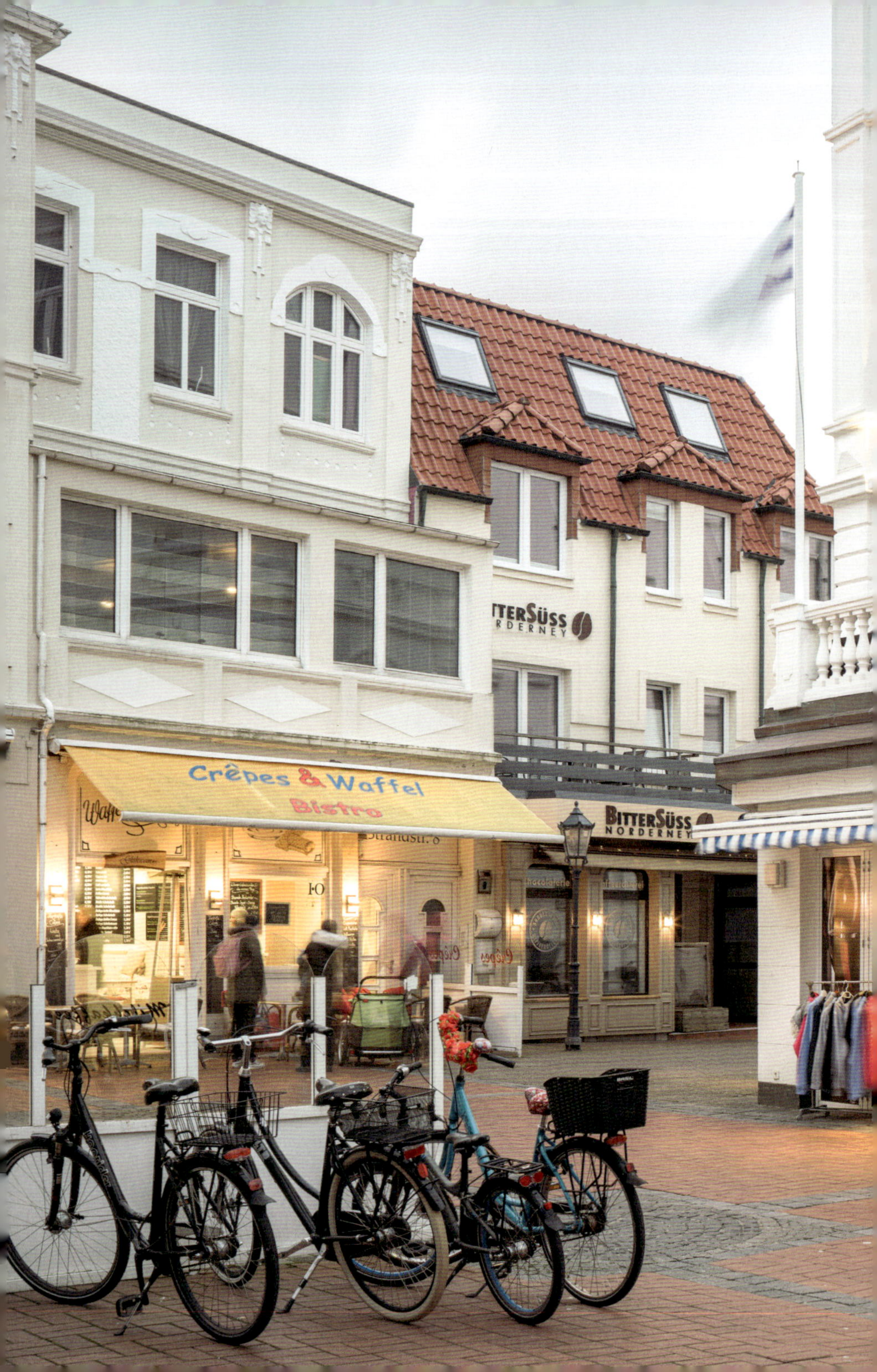
Crêpes & Waffel
Bistro
BitterSüss
Norderney

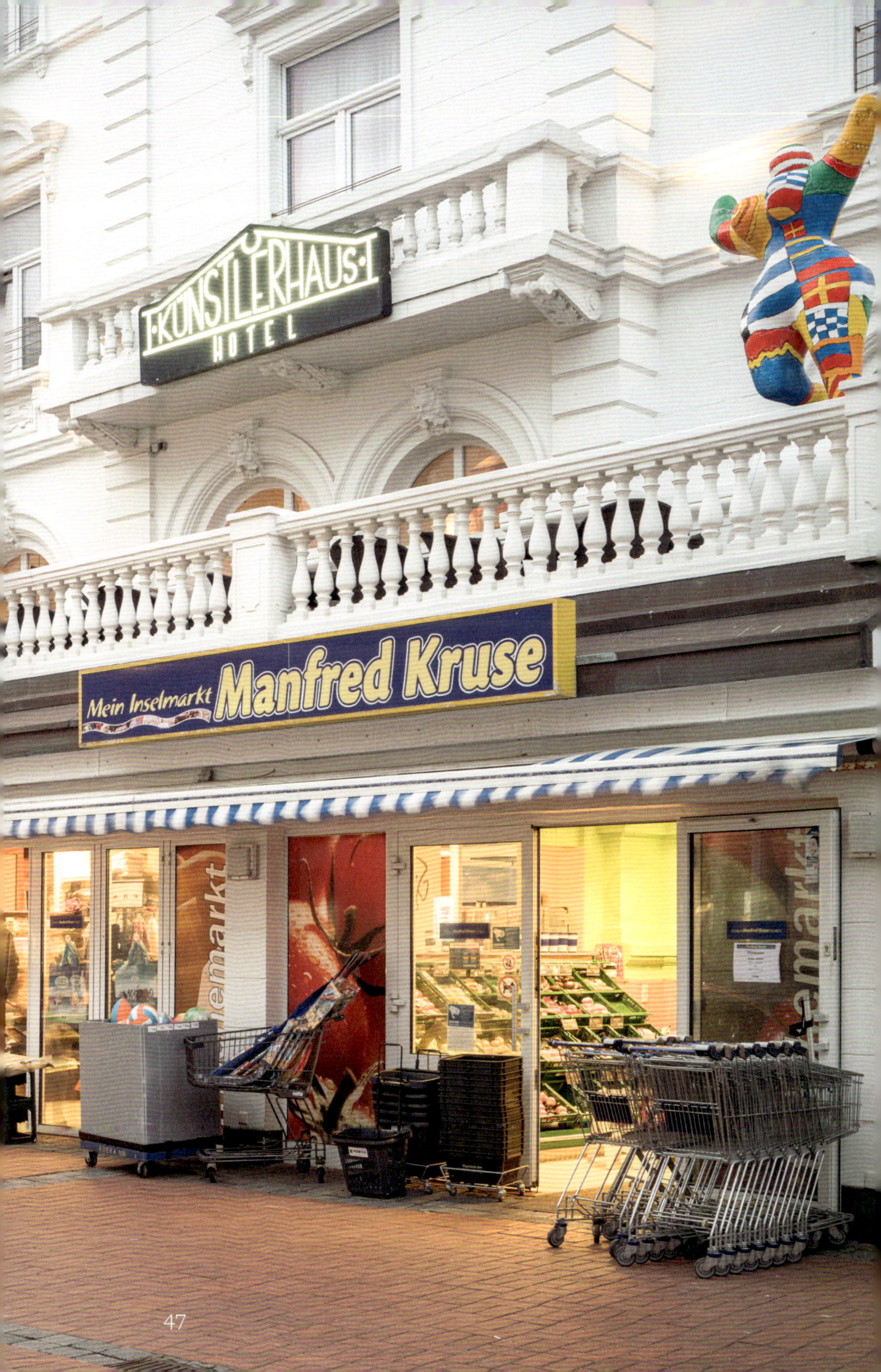
KÜNSTLERHAUS
HOTEL
Mein Inselmarkt Manfred Kruse

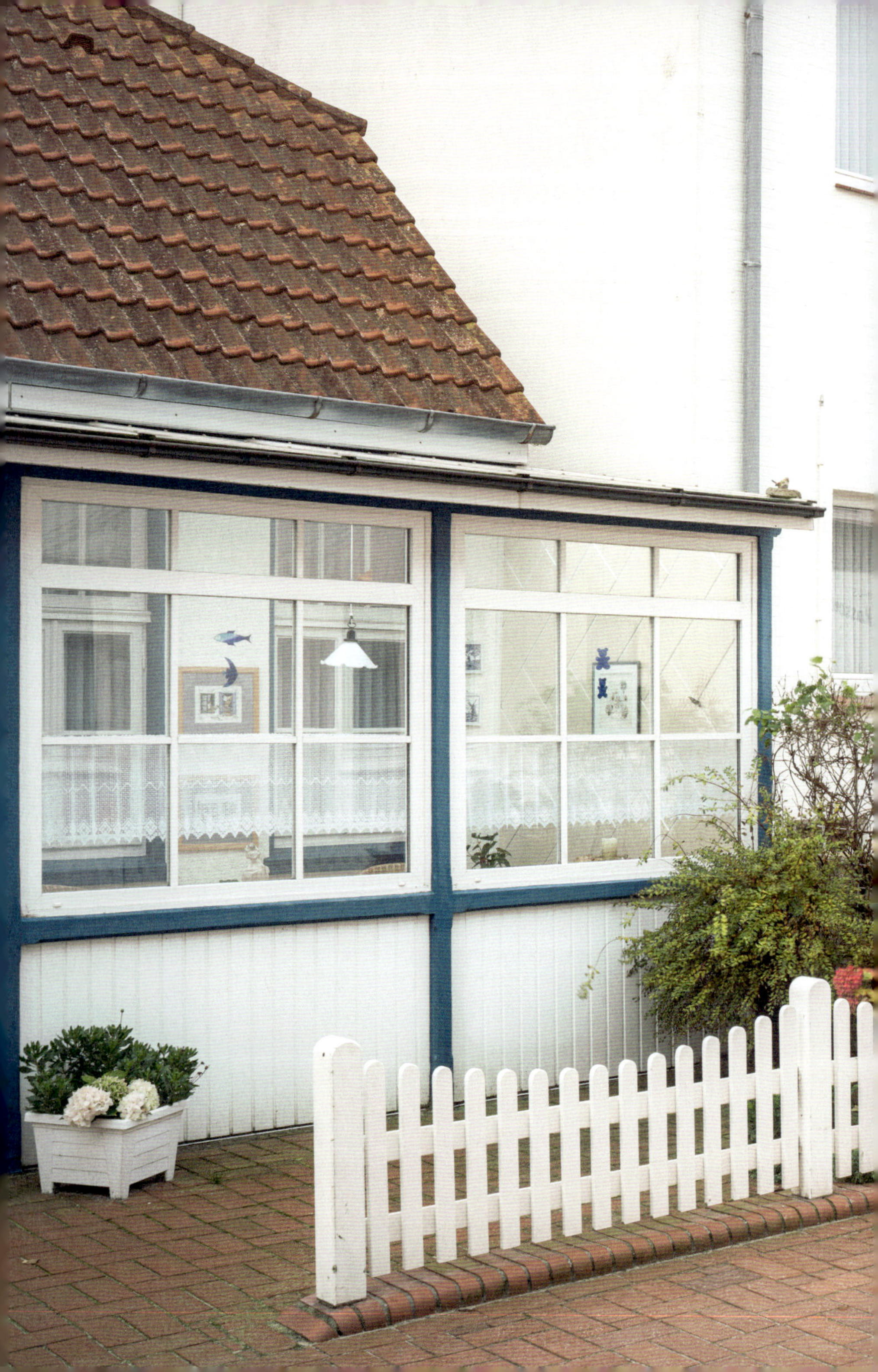

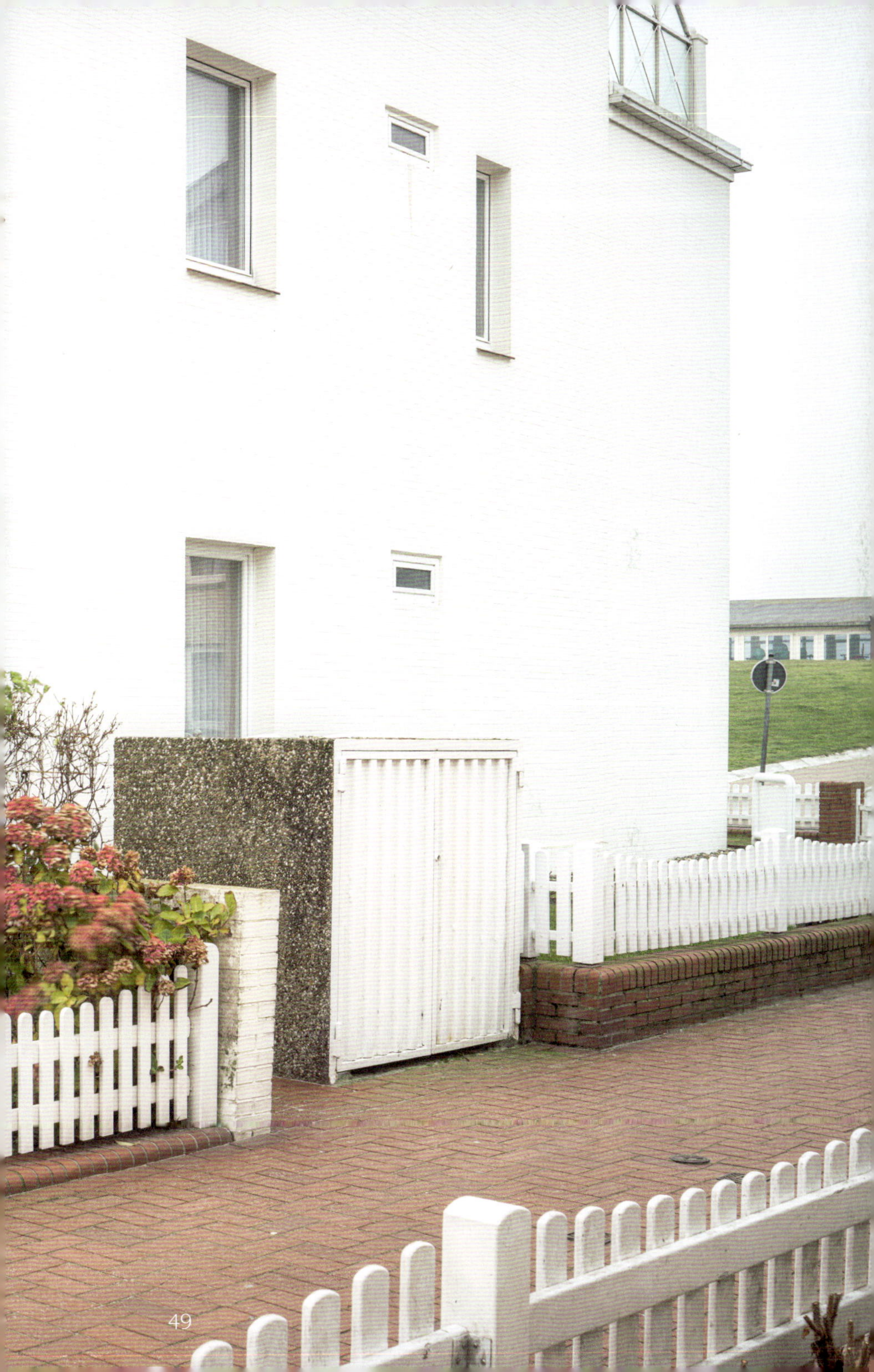

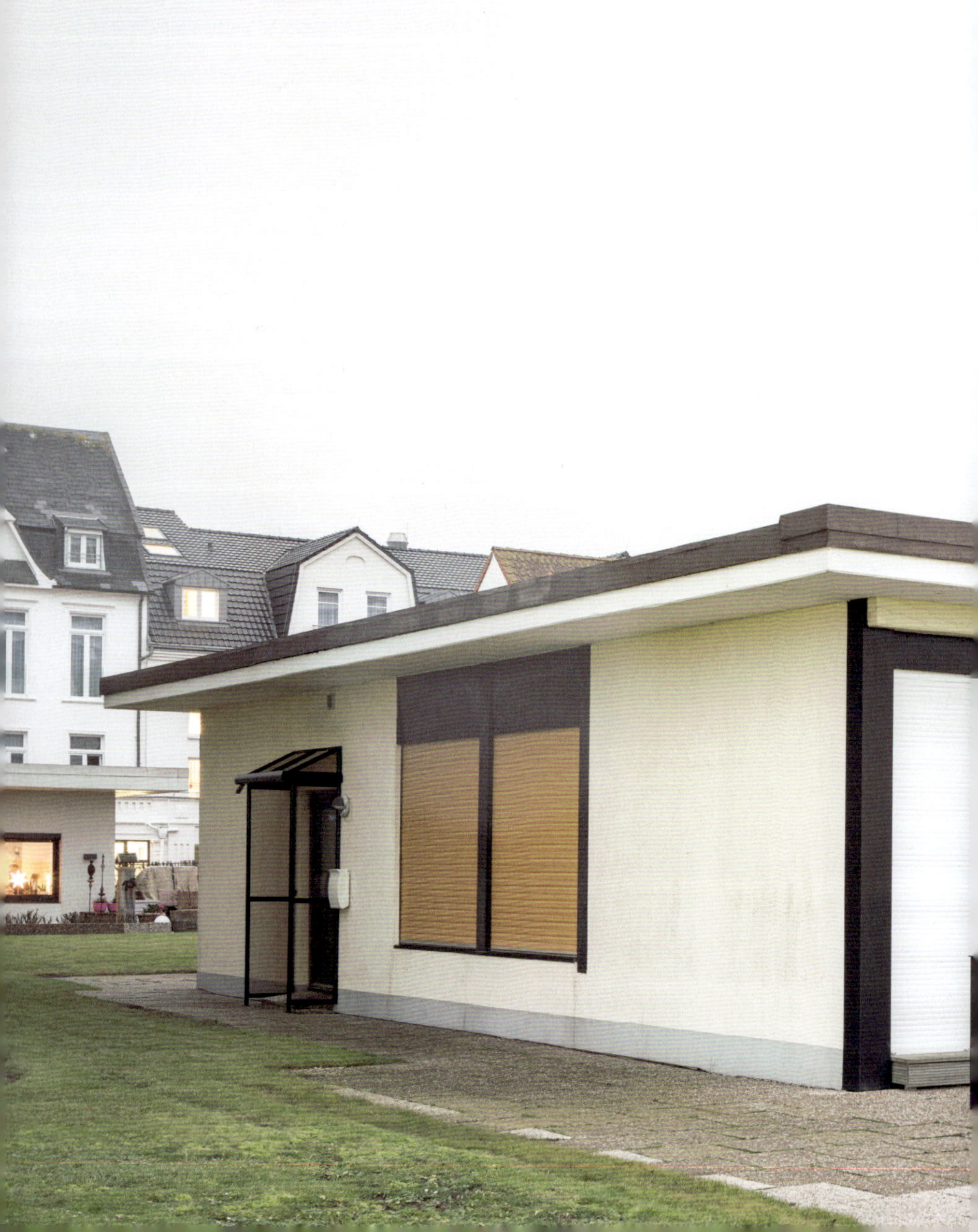

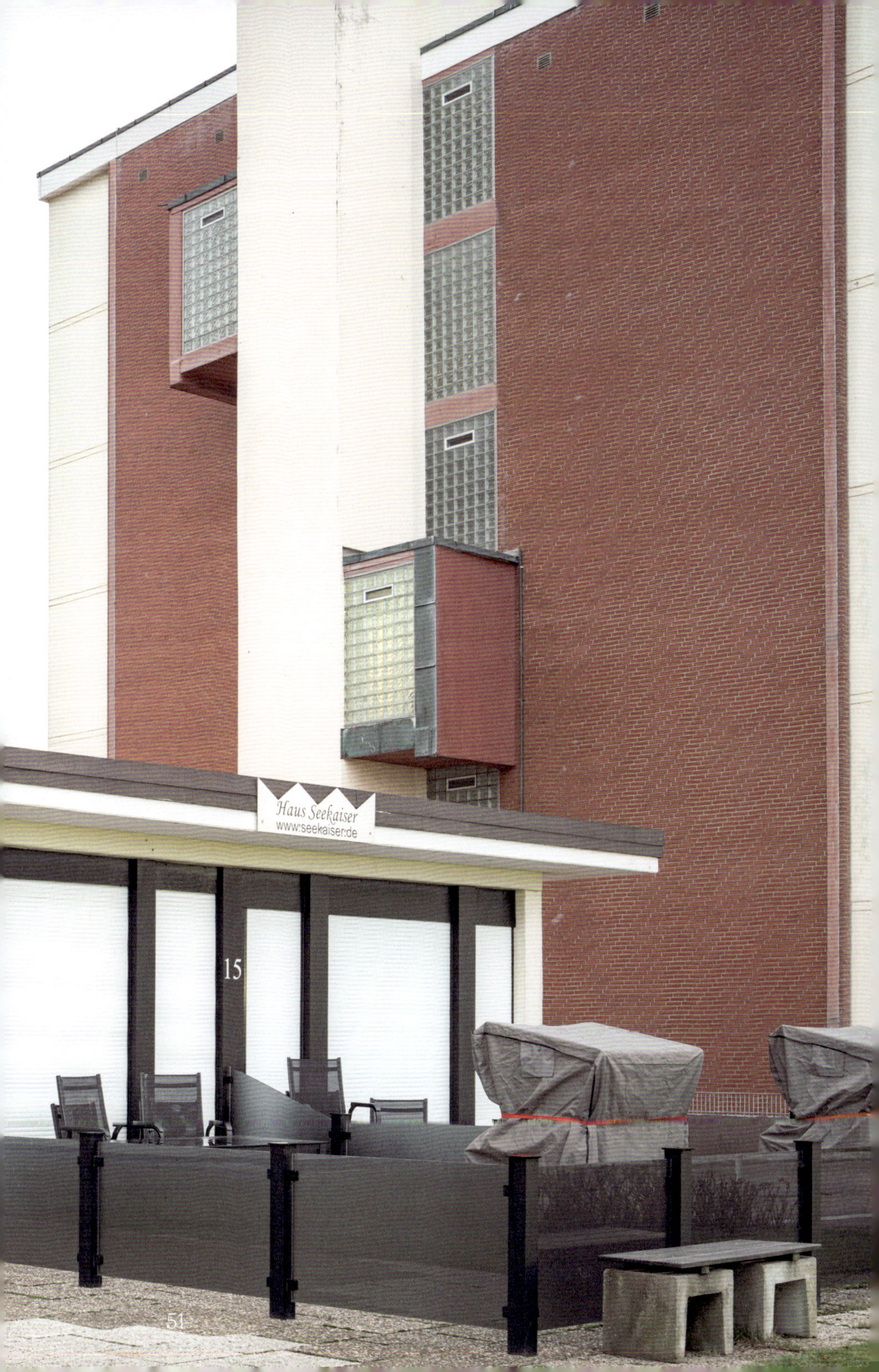
Haus Seekaiser
www.seekaiser.de
15

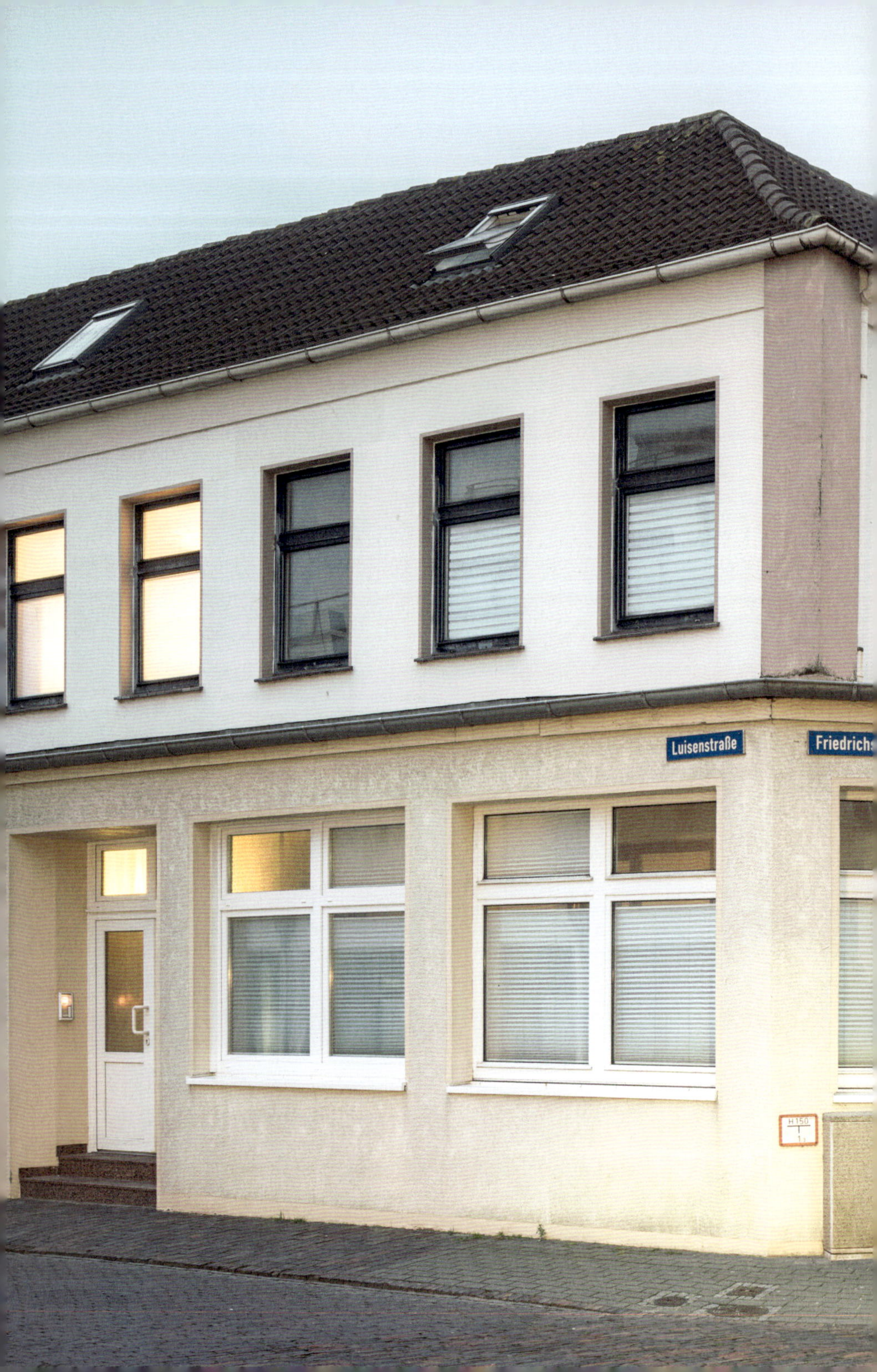
Luisenstraße
Friedrichs
H150

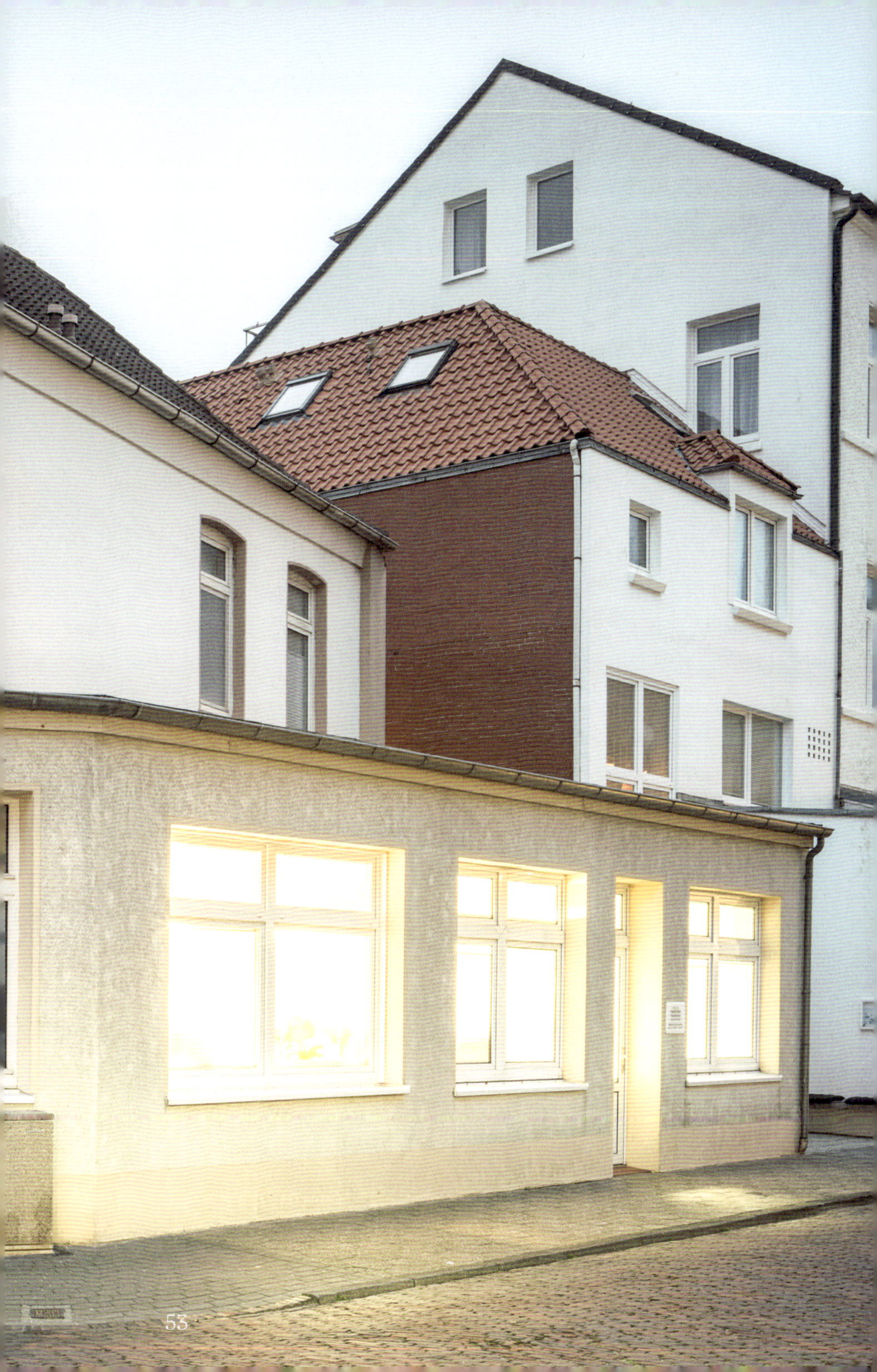

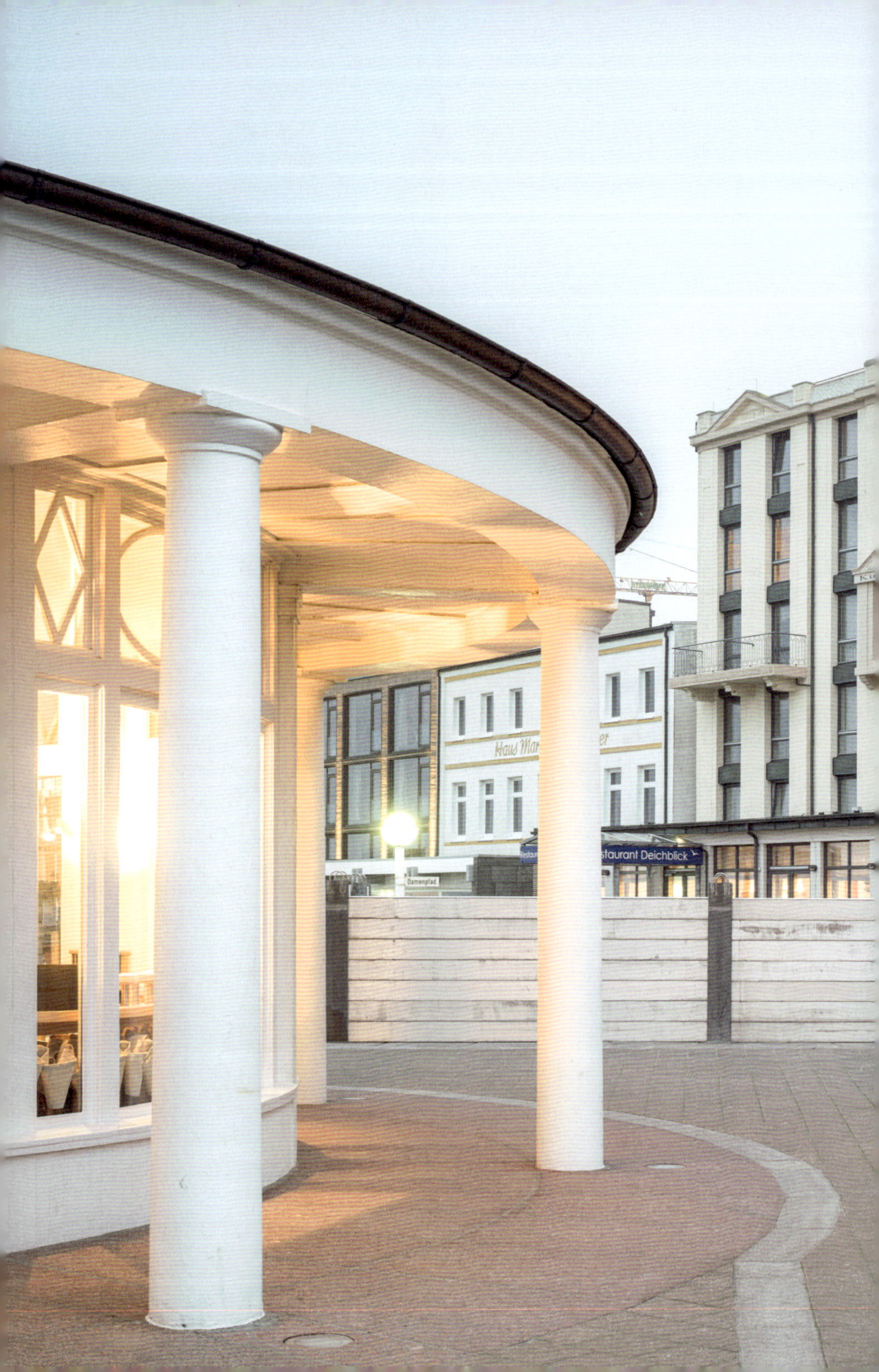
staurant Deichblick
Damenpfad

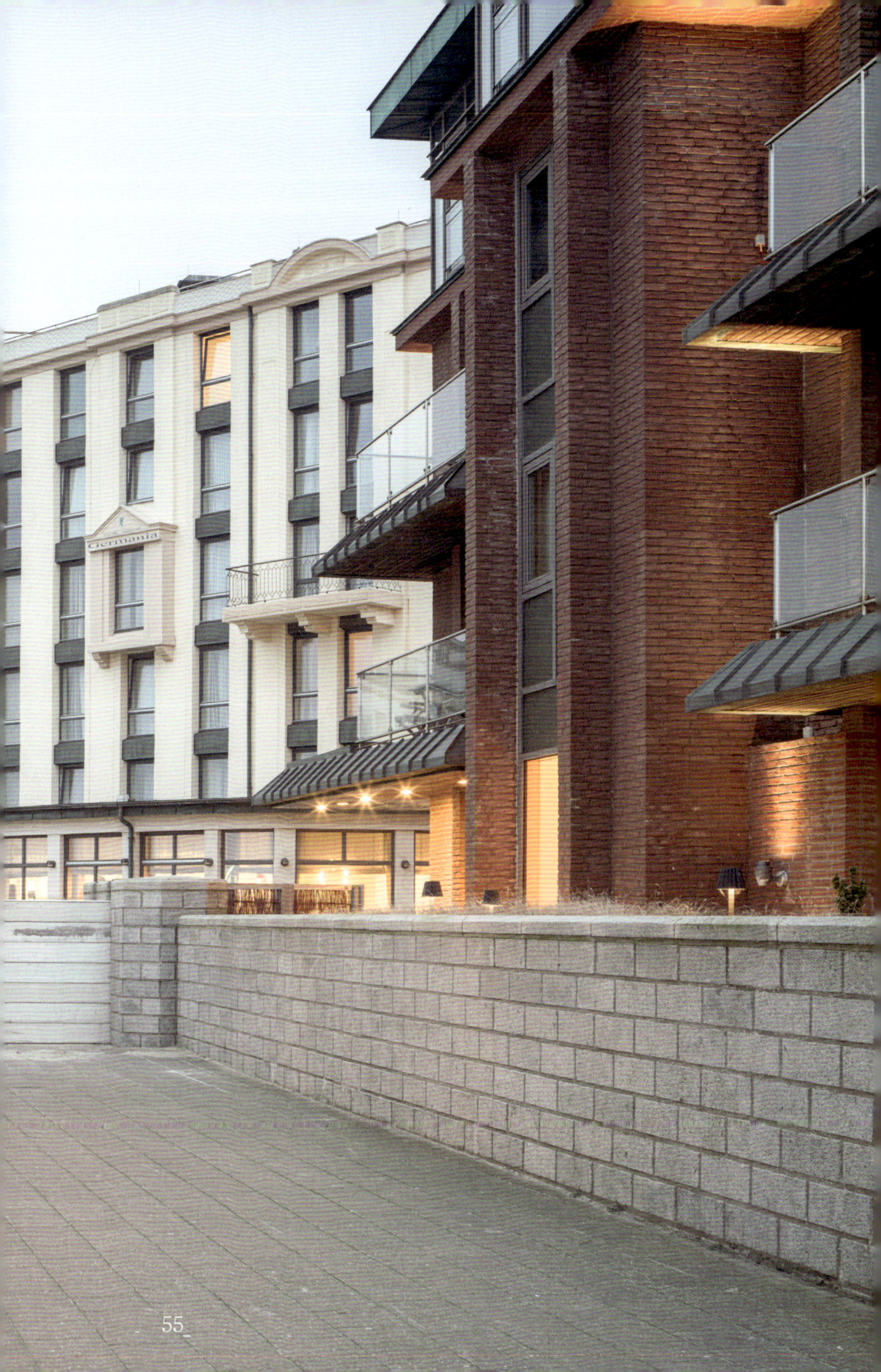
Germania

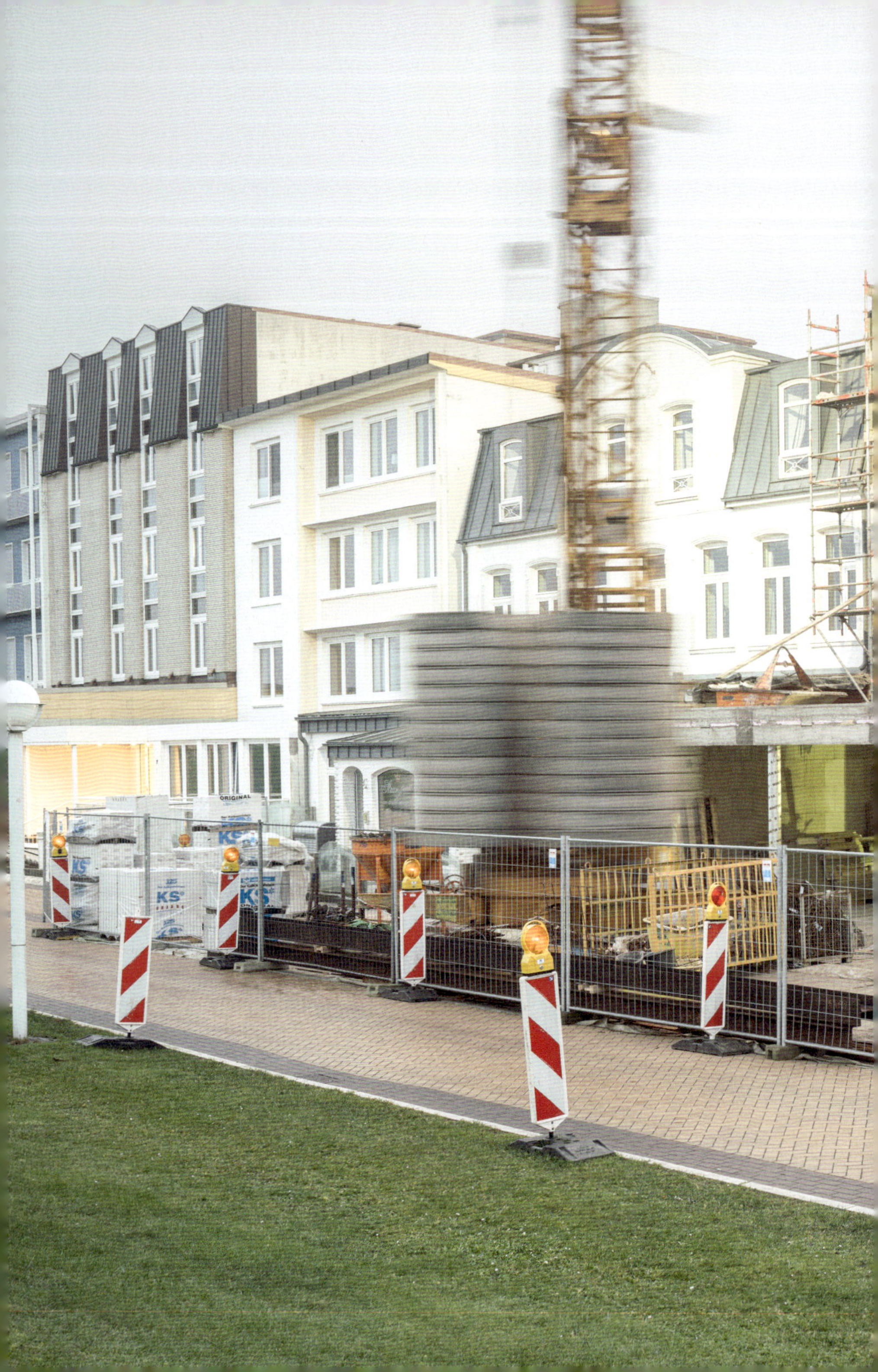
ORIGINAL
KS

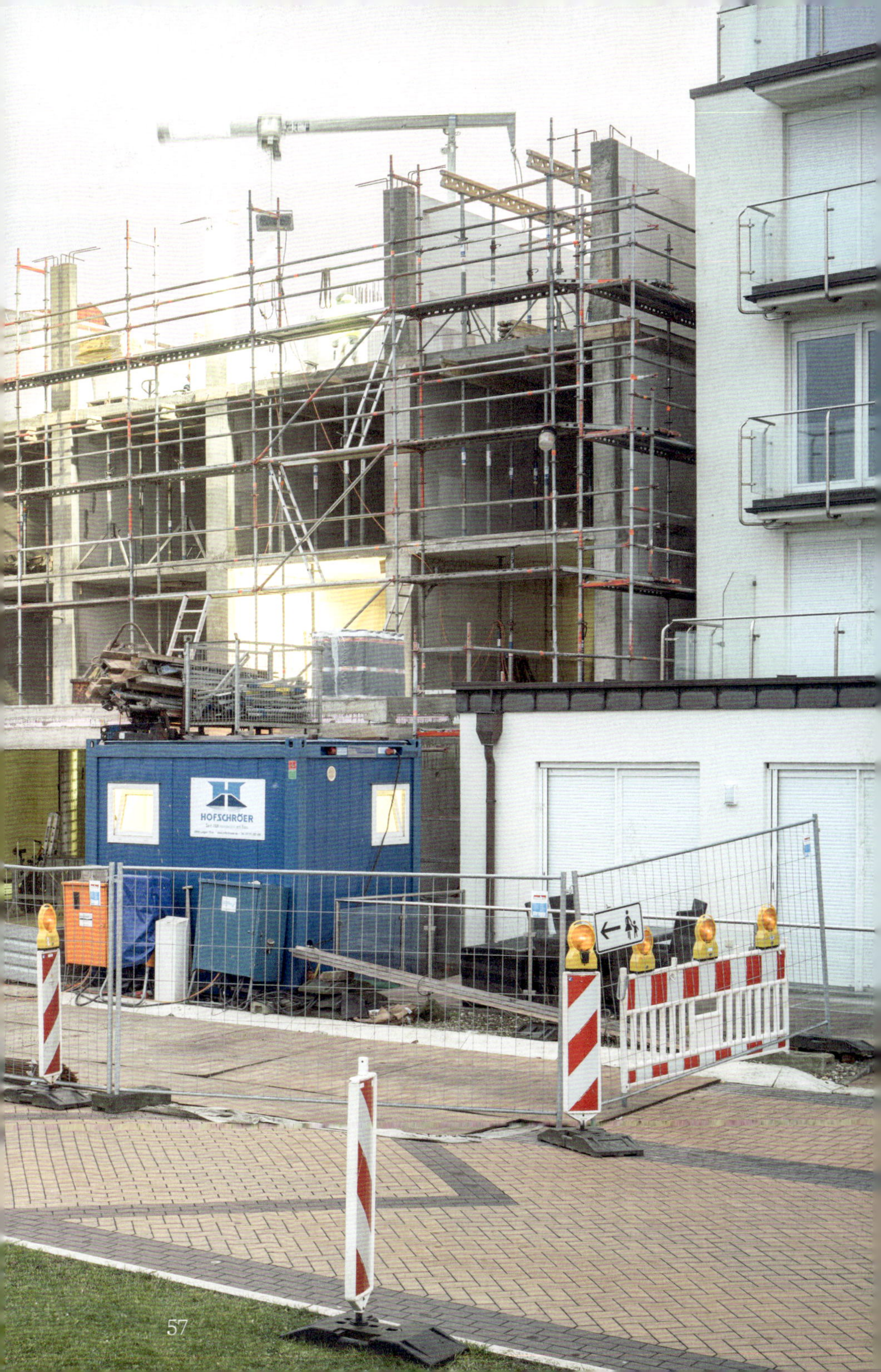
HOFSCHRÖER

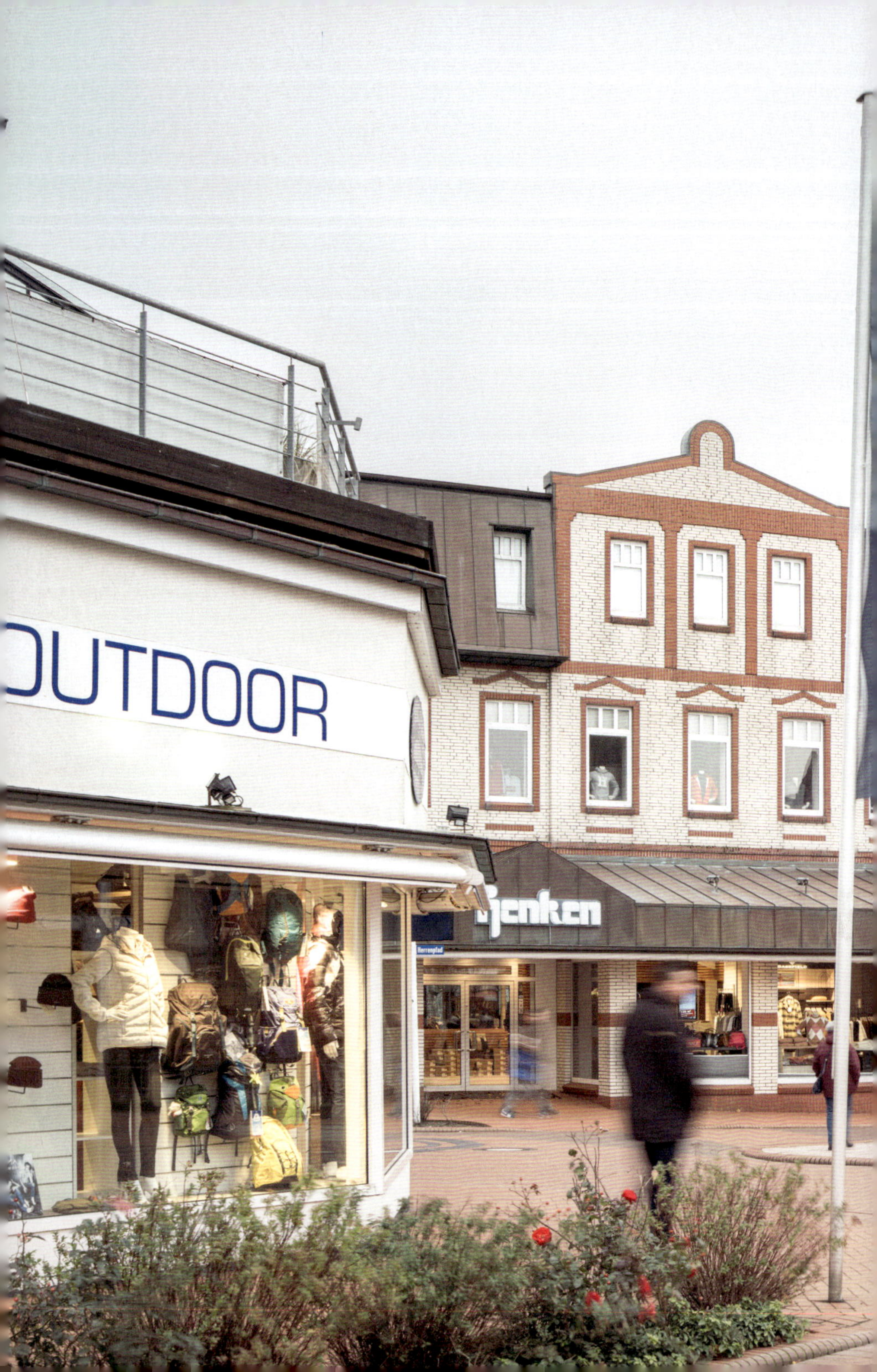
OUTDOOR
Herrenpfad

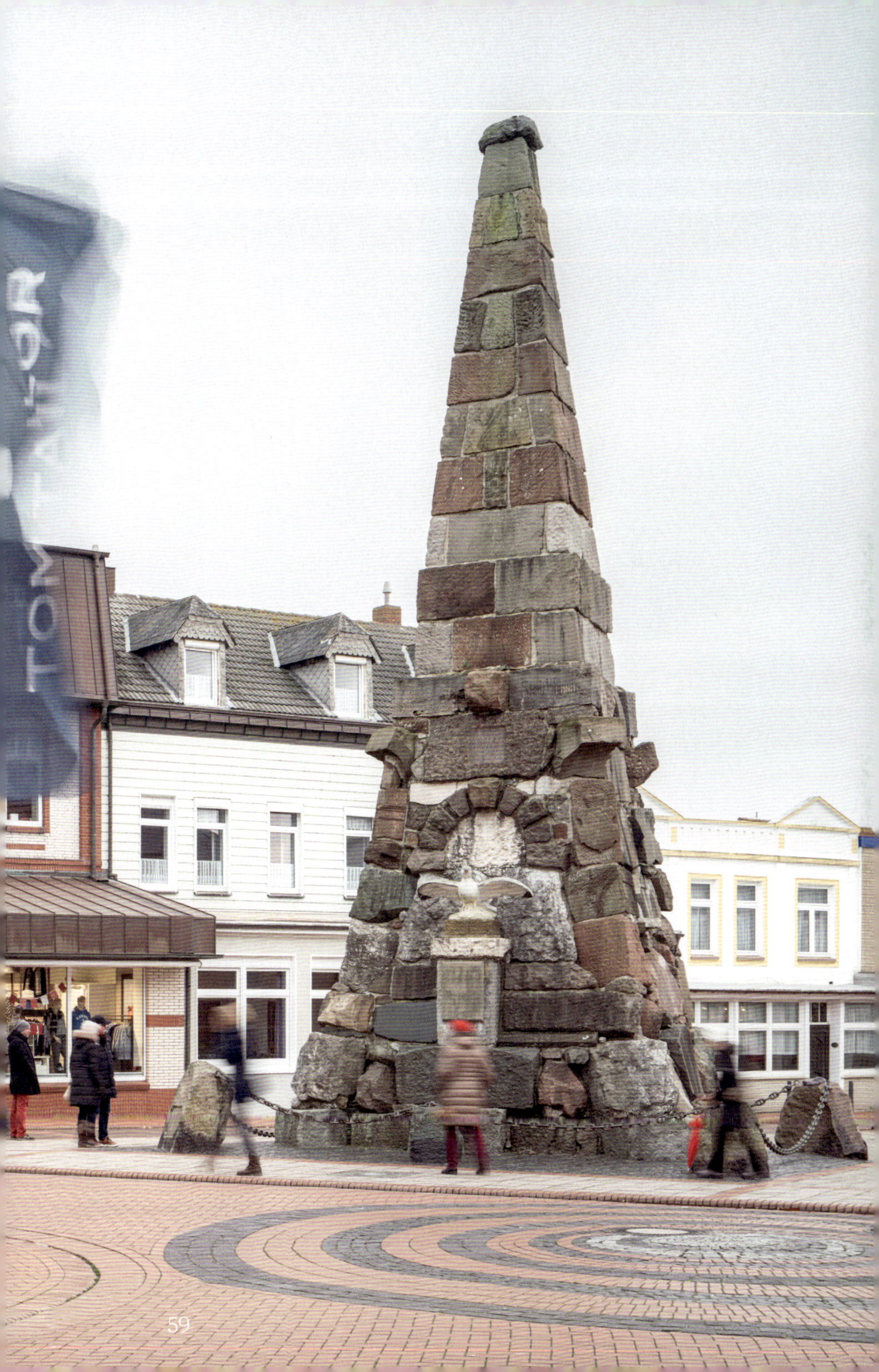
TOM TAILOR

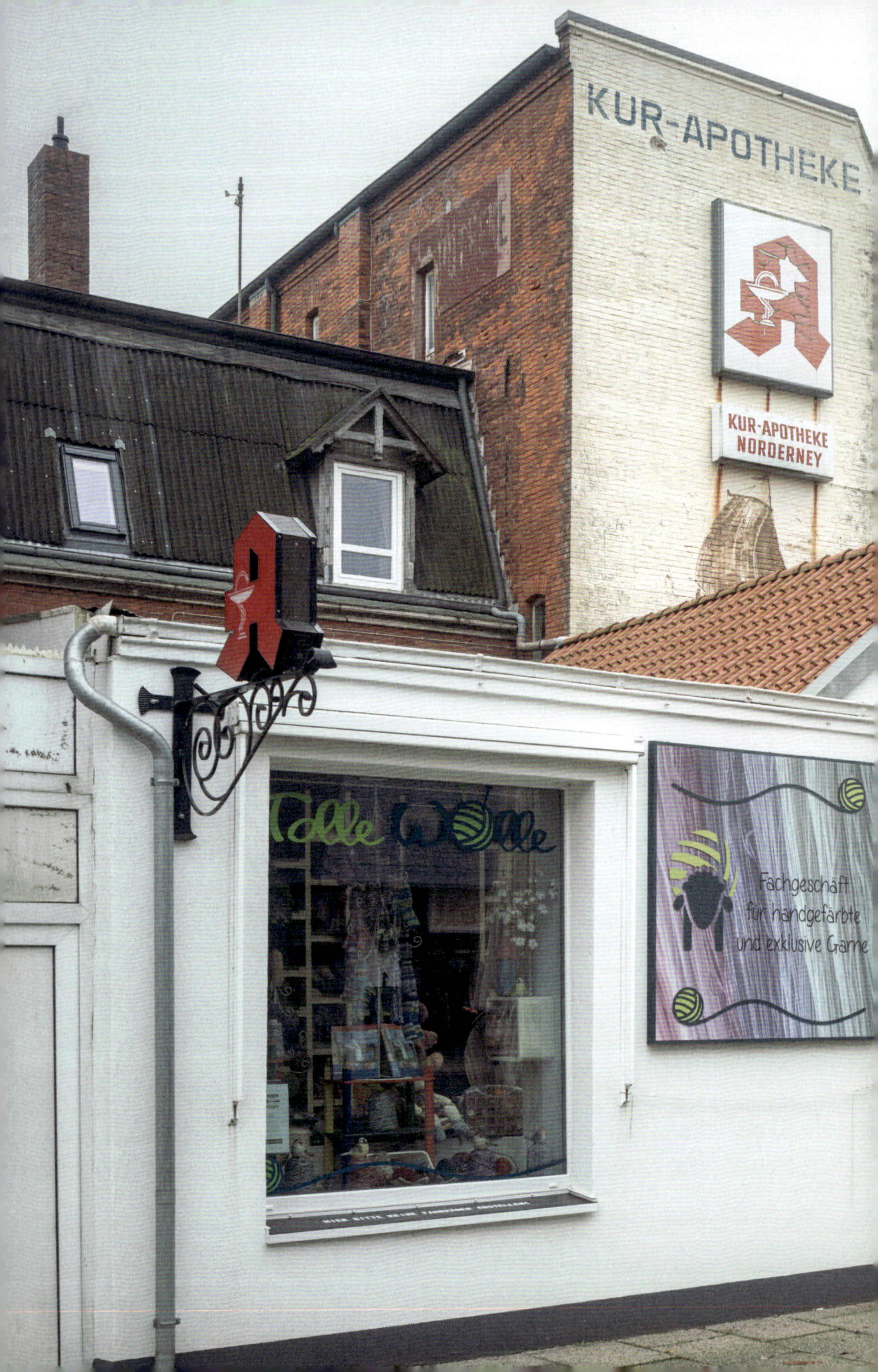
KUR-APOTHEKE
KUR-APOTHEKE
NORDERNEY
Tolle Wolle
Fachgeschäft
für handgefärbte
und exklusive Garne

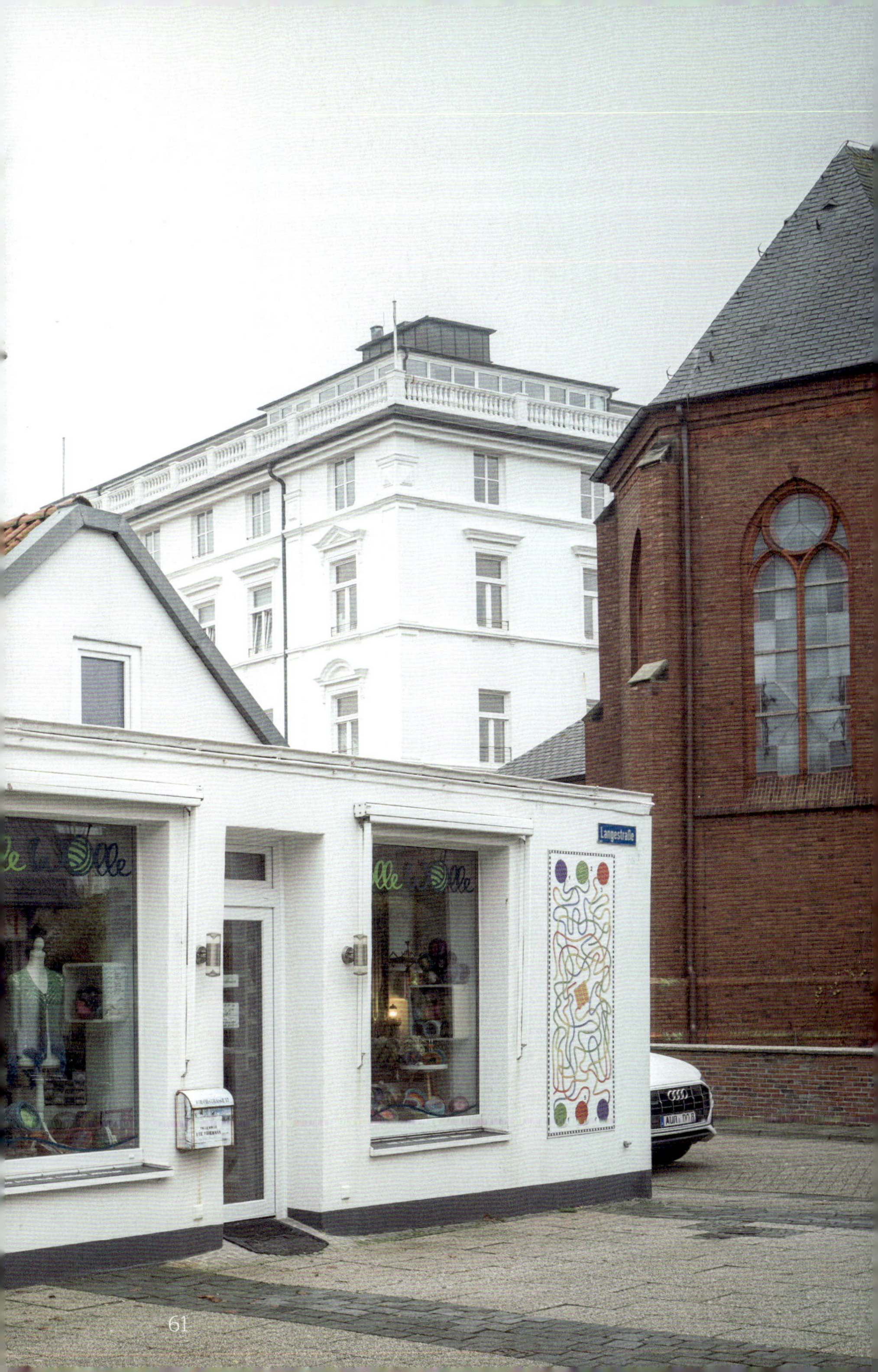
Langestraße

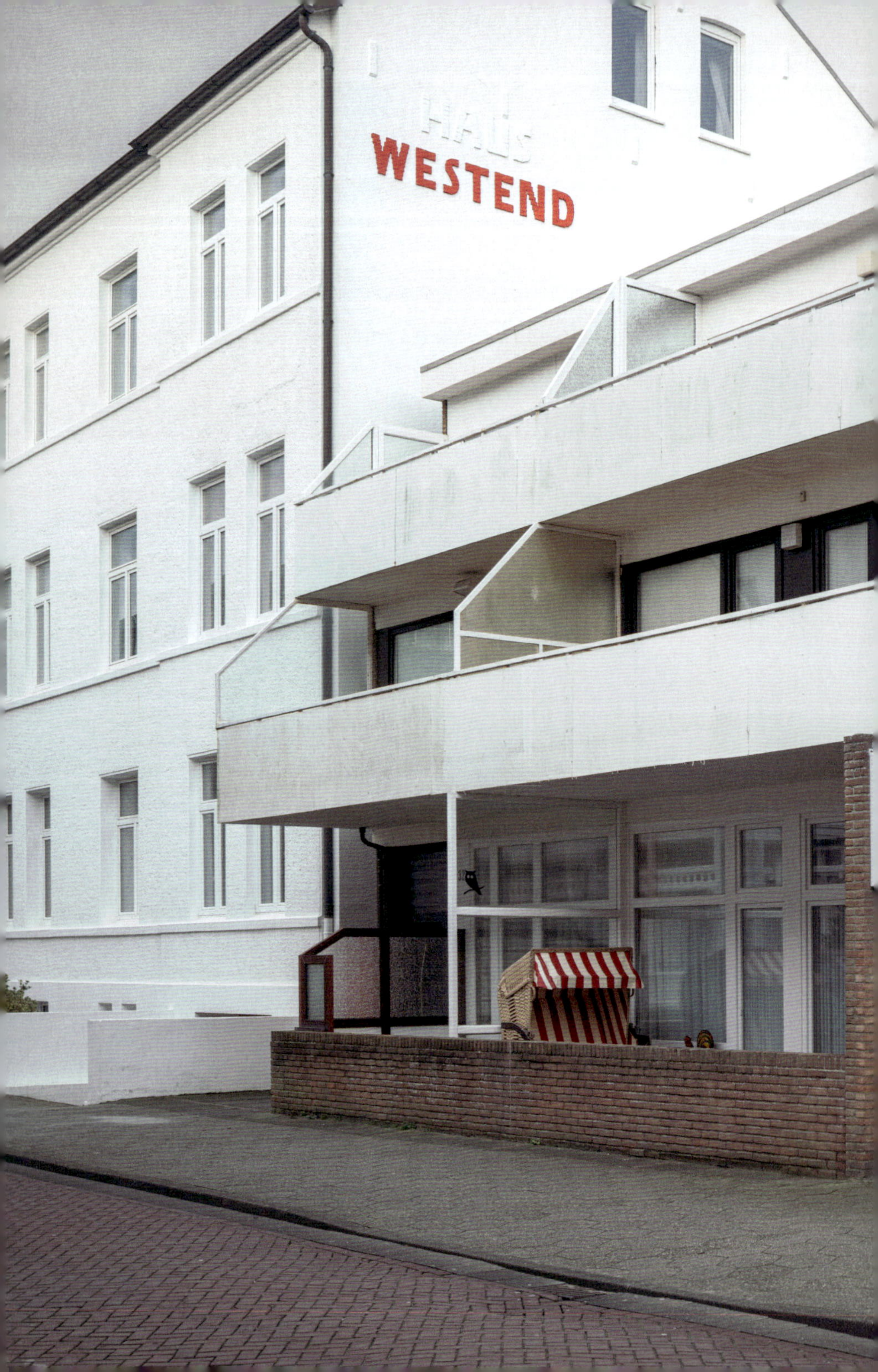
HAUS
WESTEND

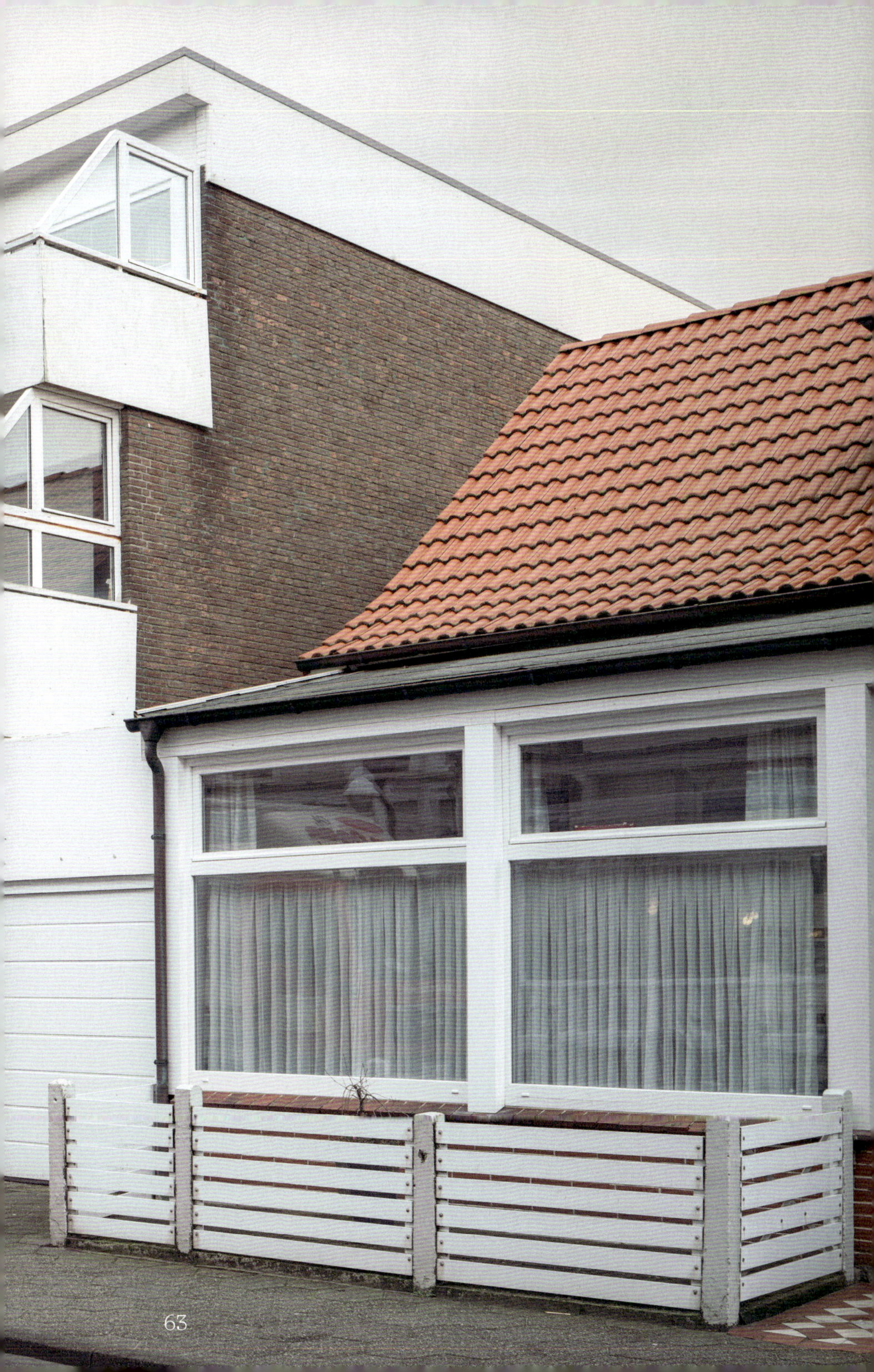

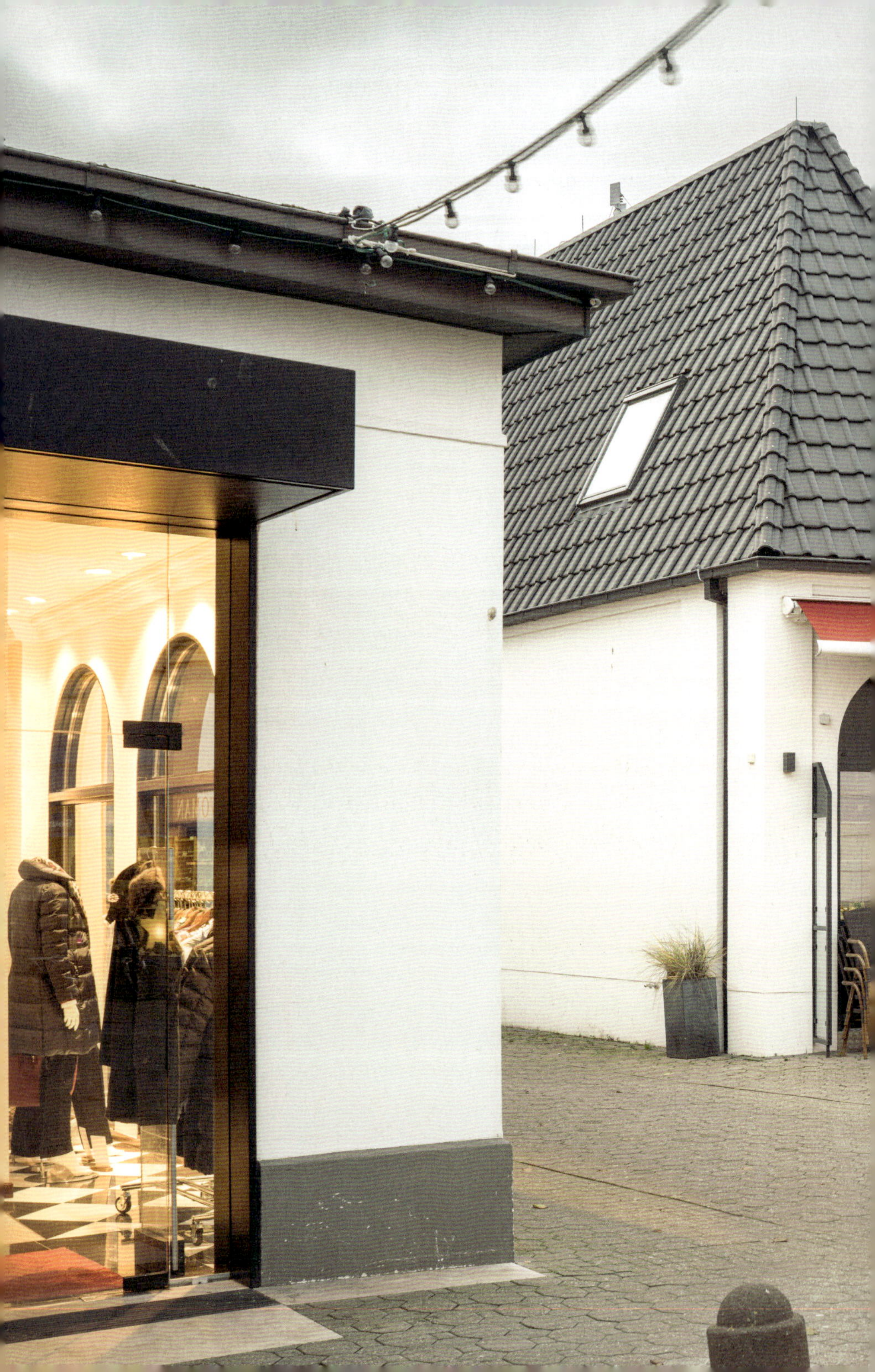

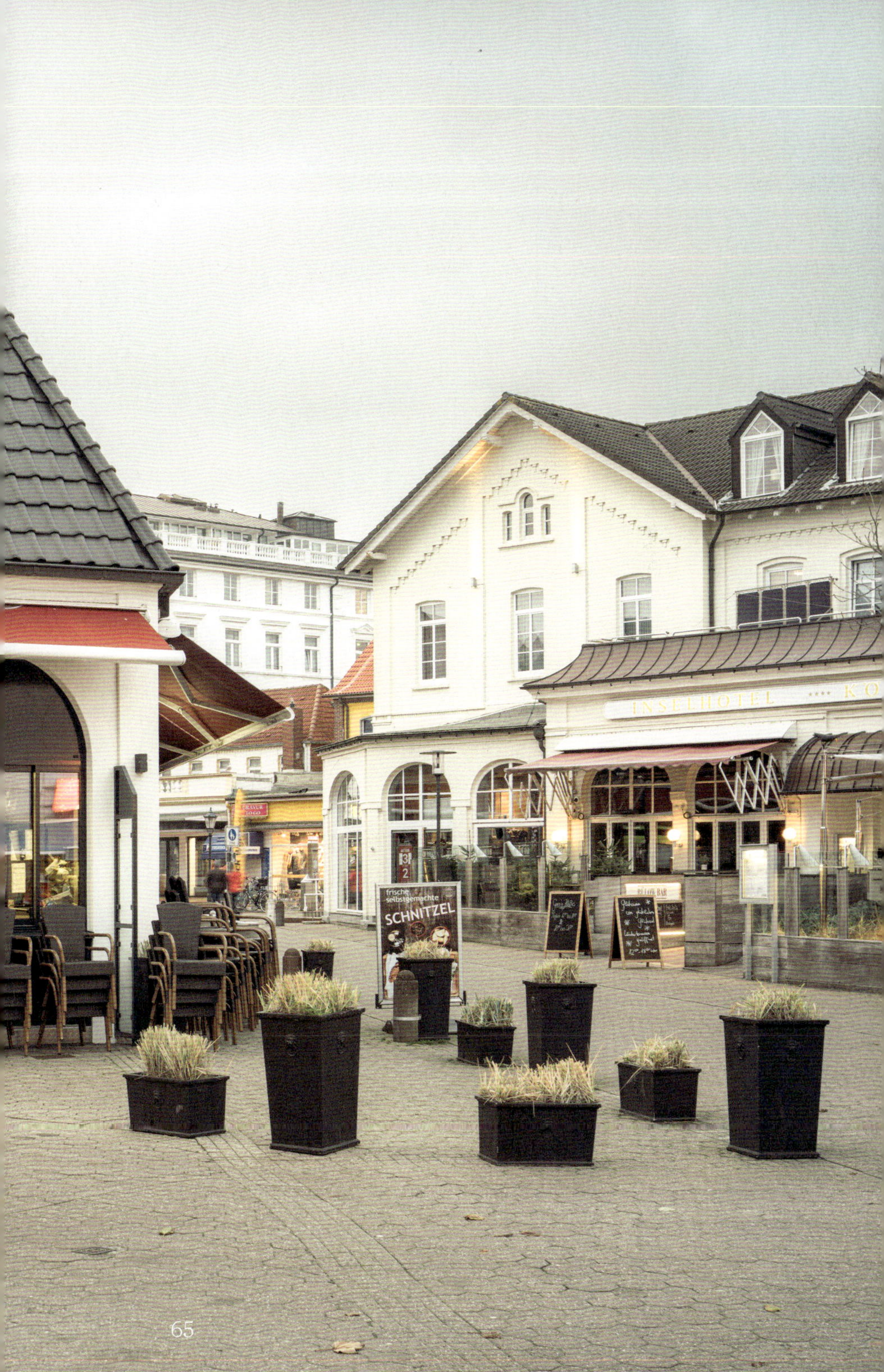
INSELHOTEL
frische
selbstgemachte
SCHNITZEL

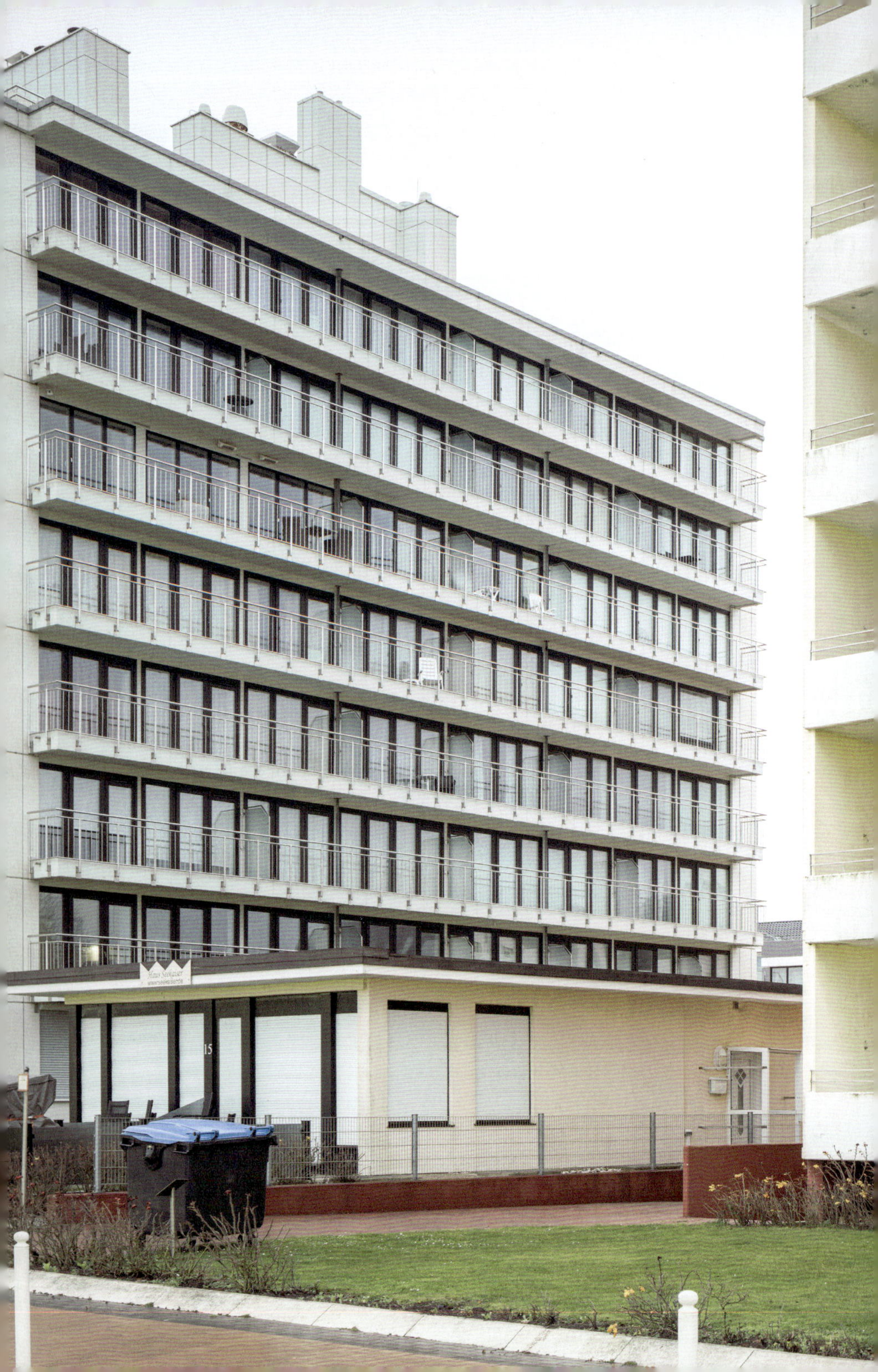
Haus Seekaiser
15

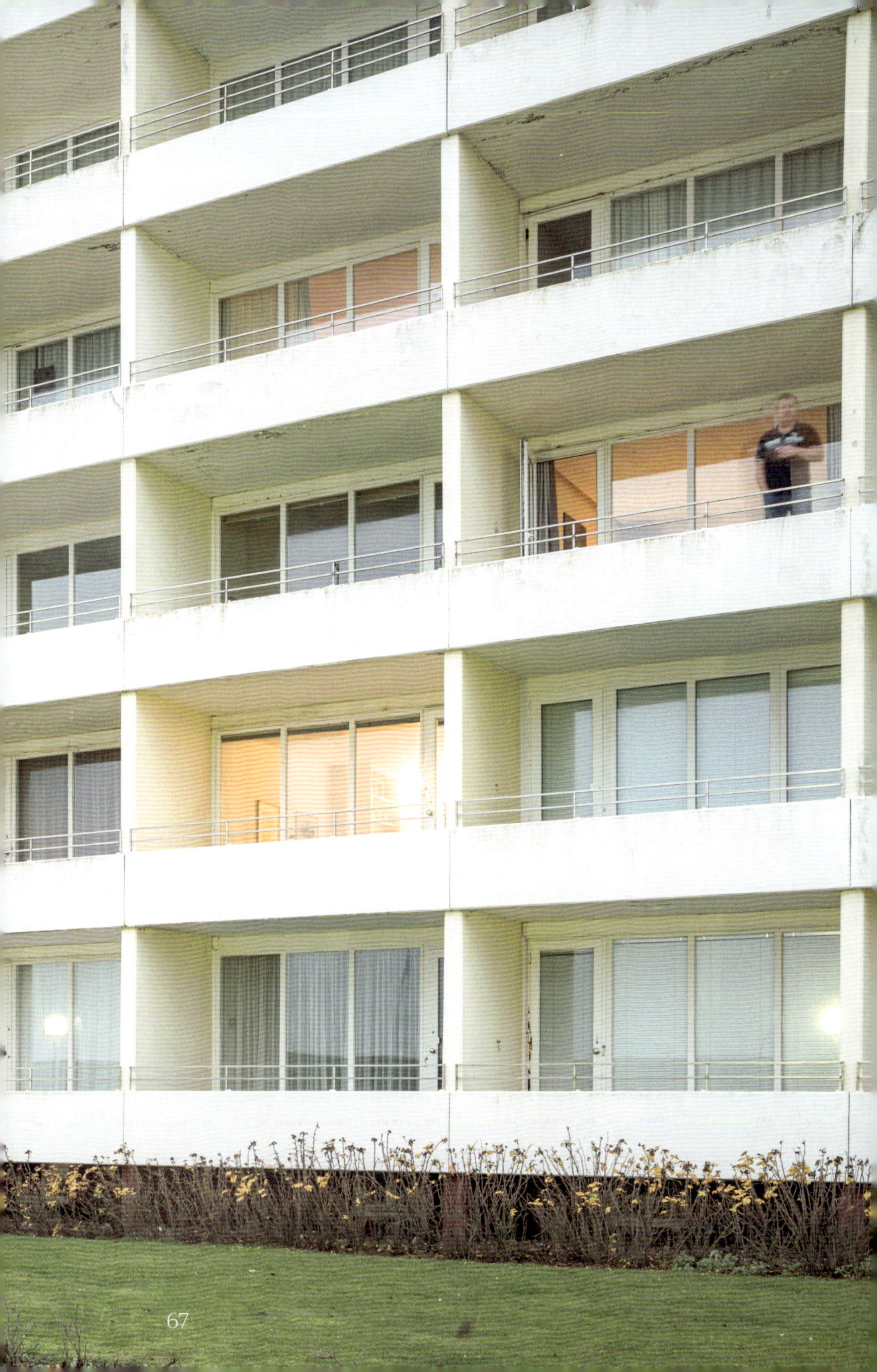

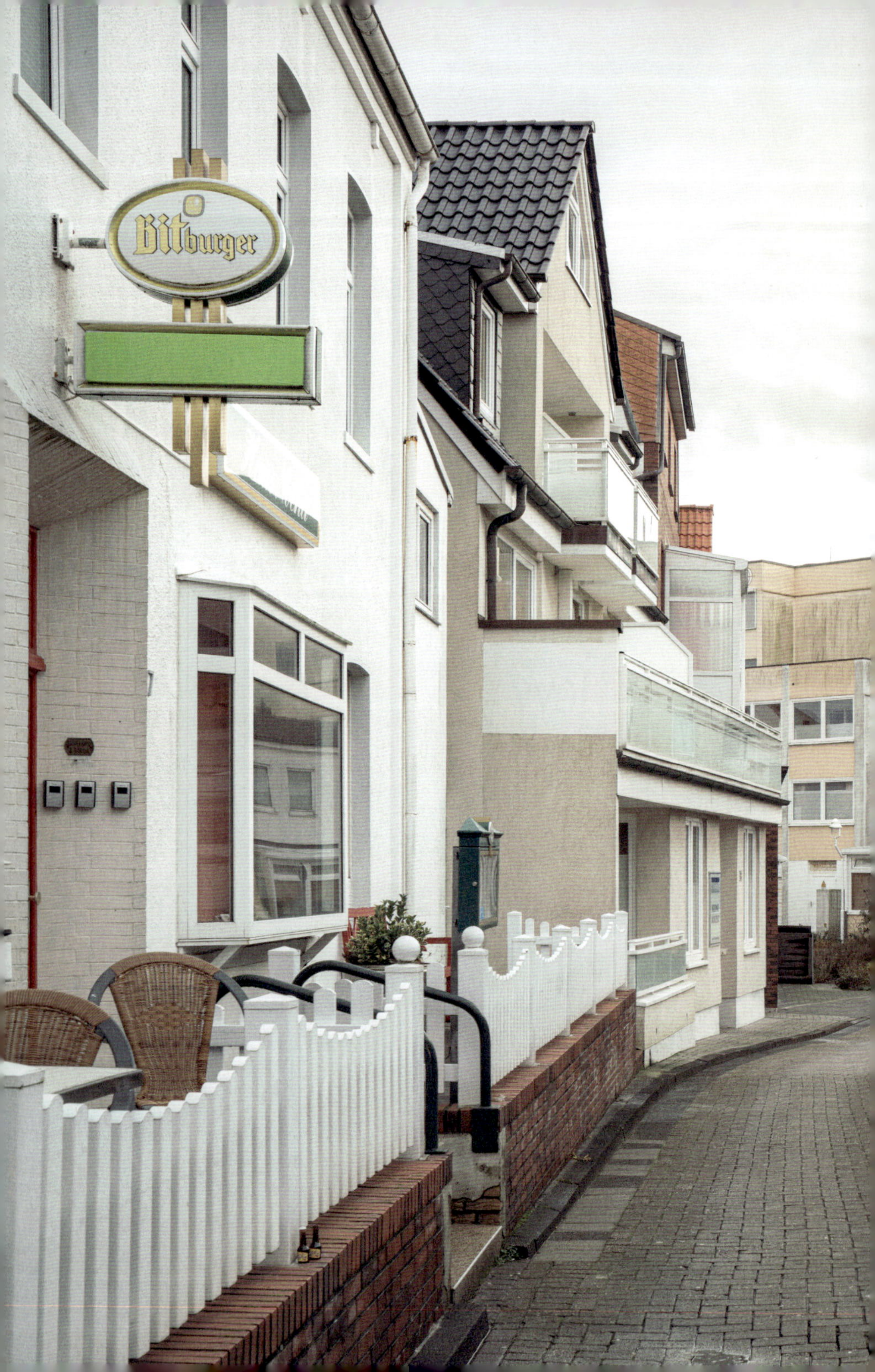
Bitburger

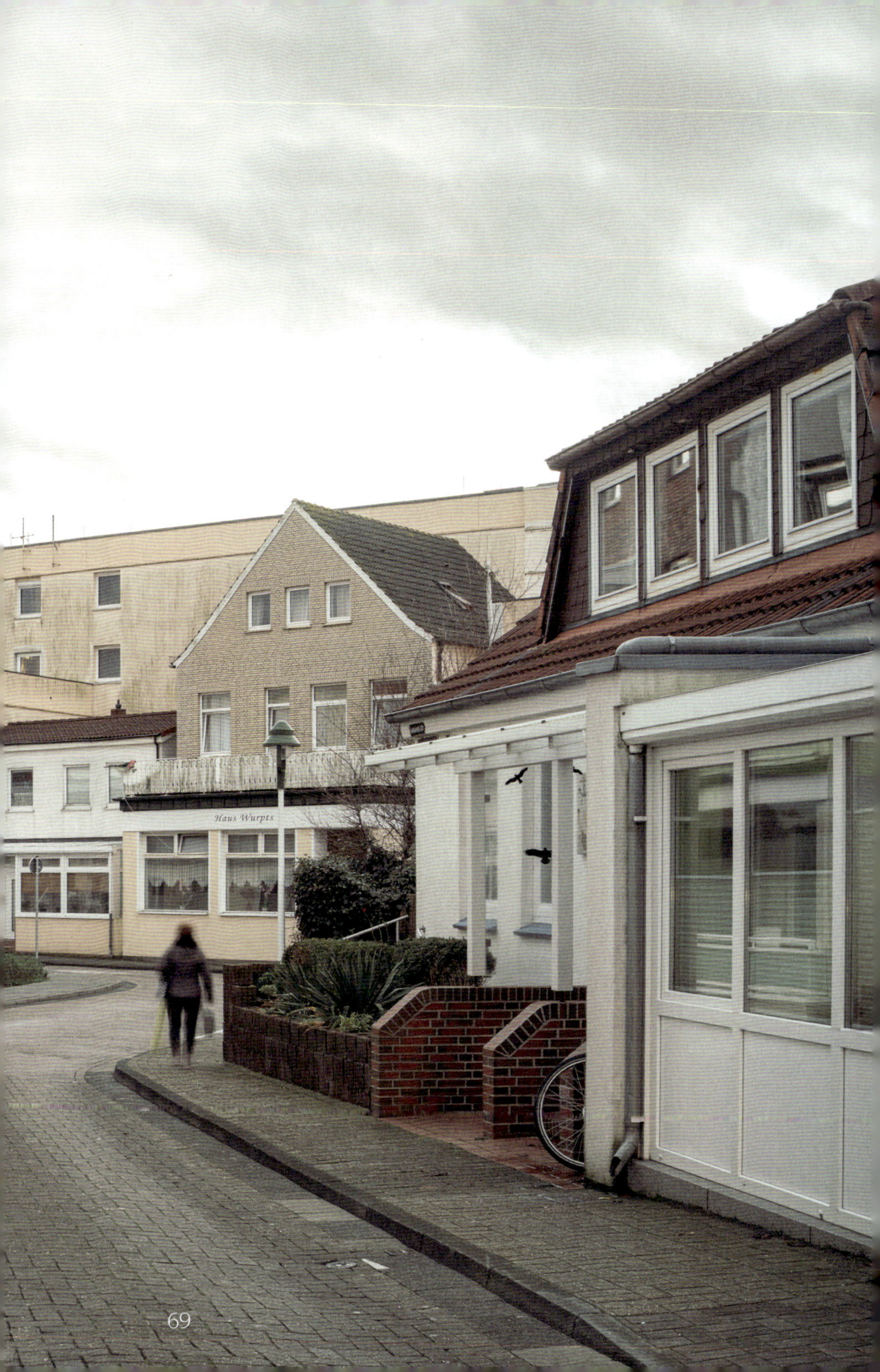
Haus Wurpts

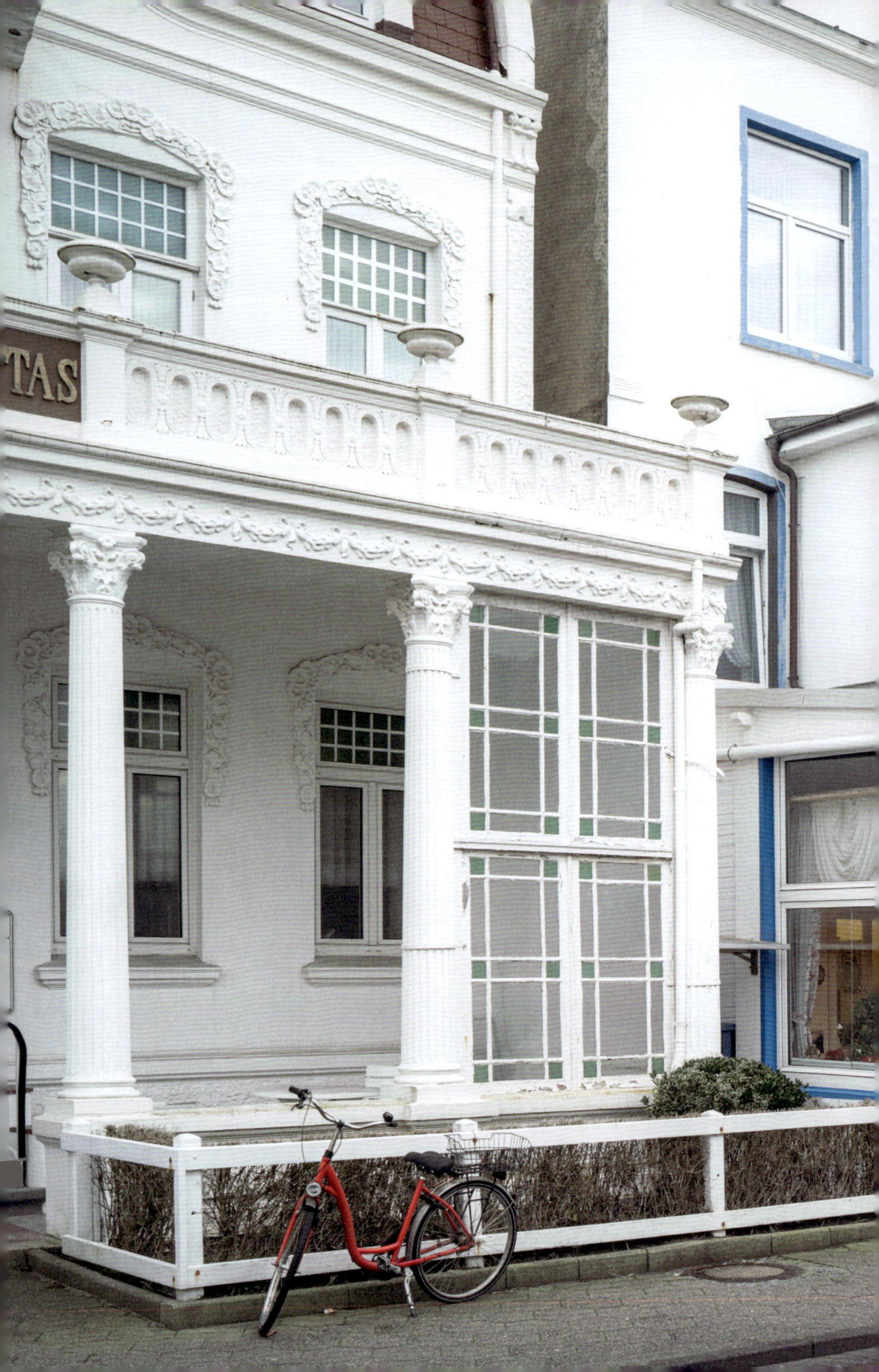
TAS

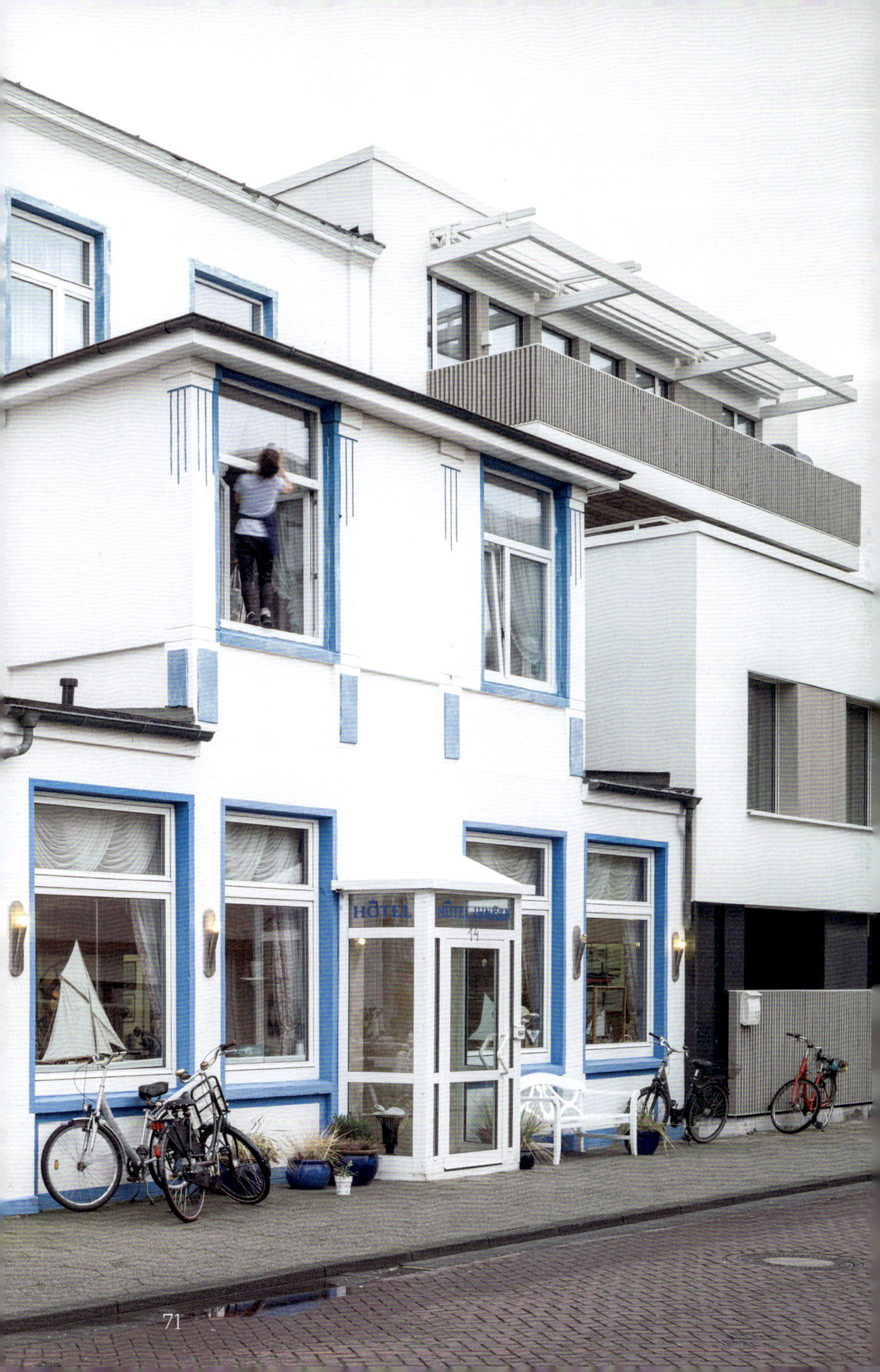
HOTEL
14

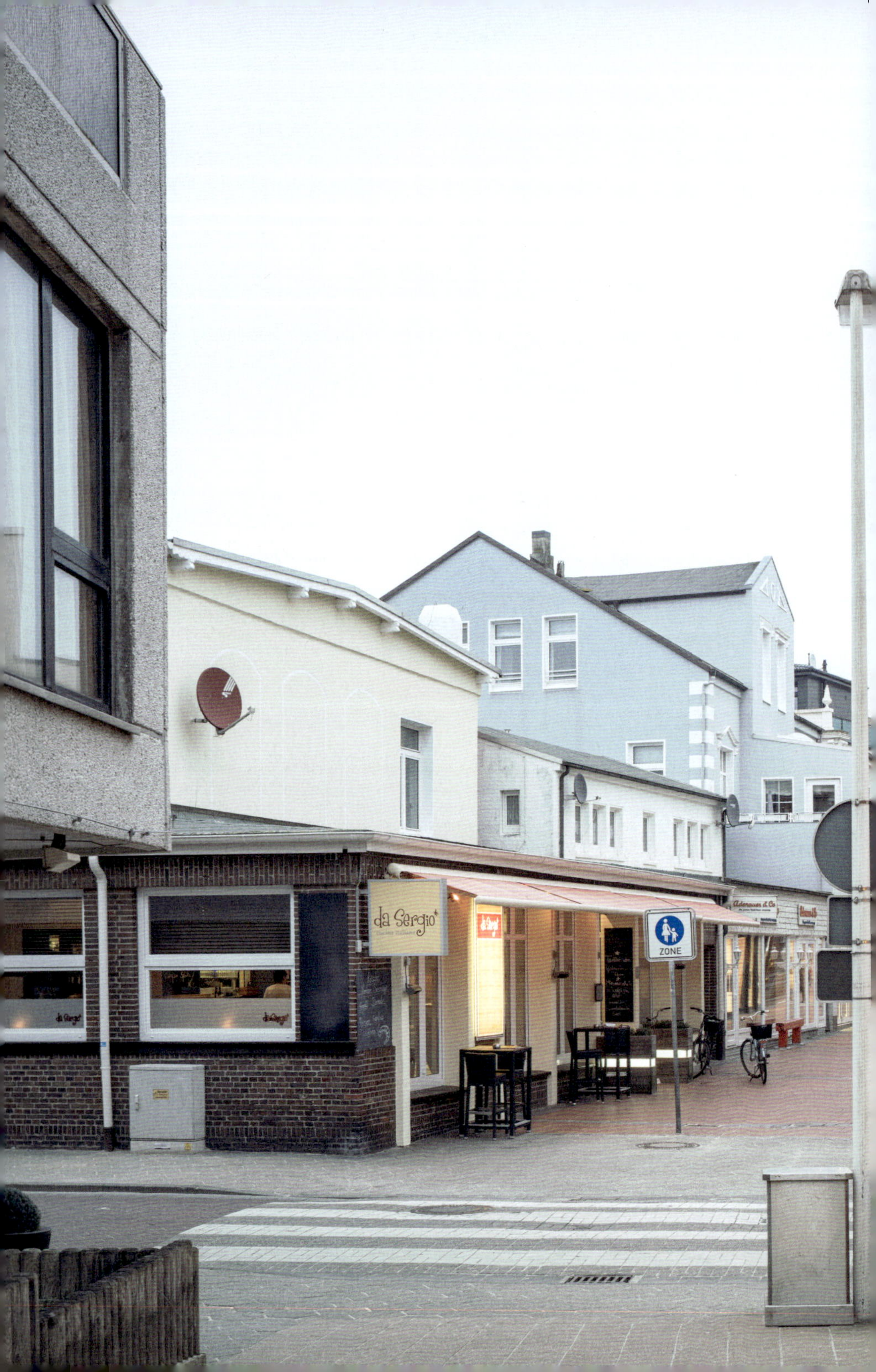
da Sergio
ZONE

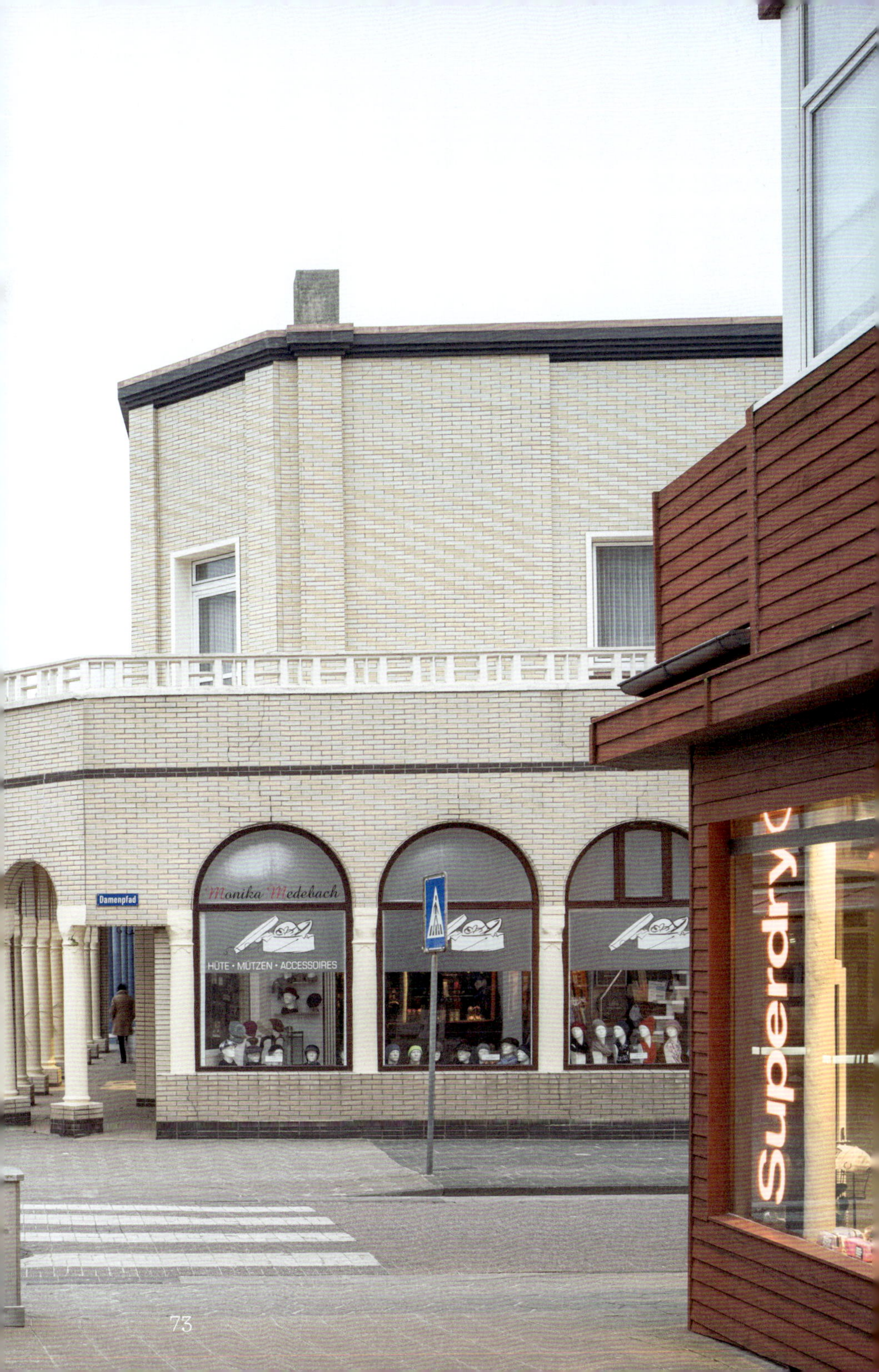
Damenpfad
Monika Medebach
HÜTE • MÜTZEN • ACCESSOIRES
Superdry

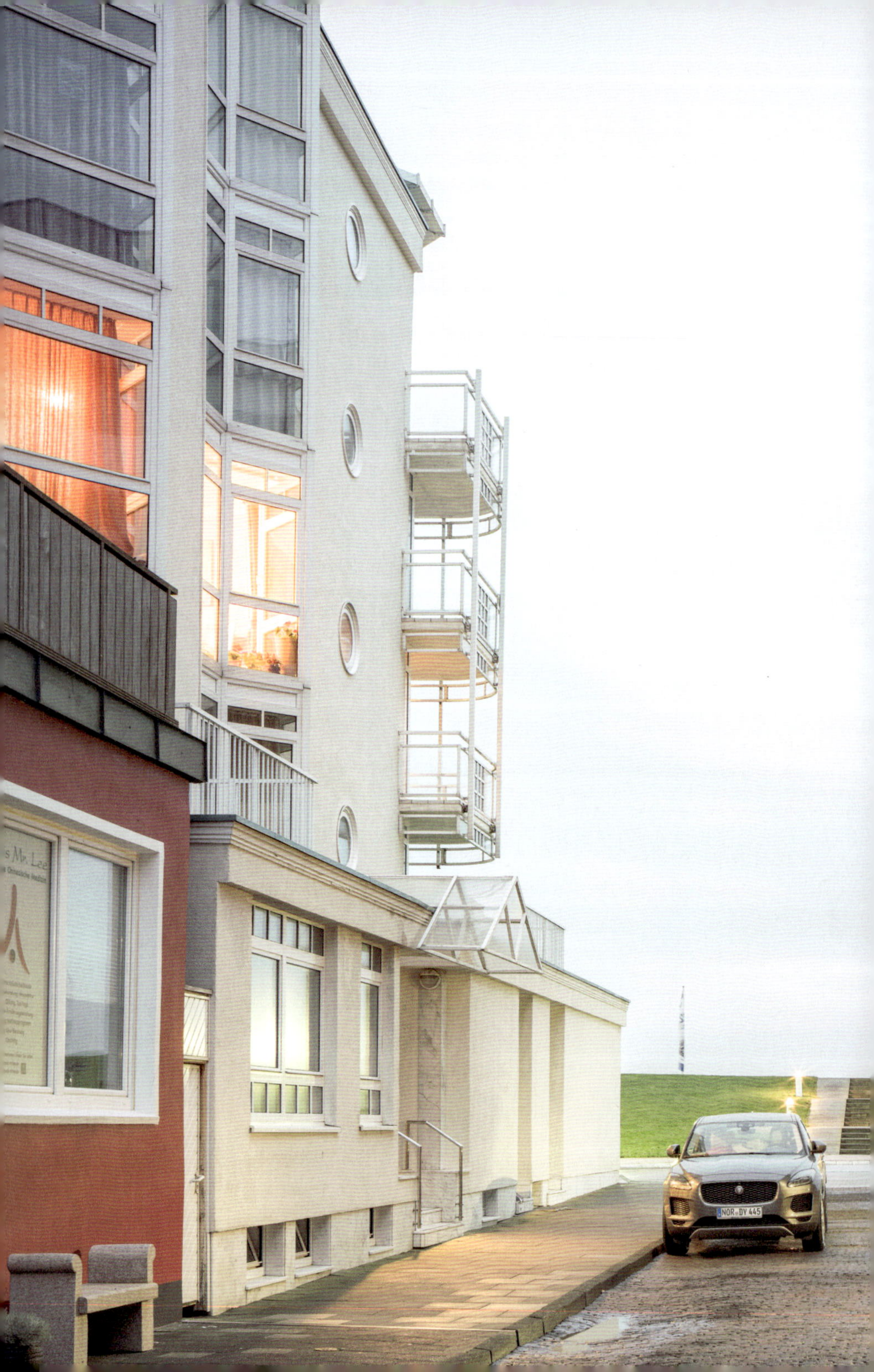
Mr. Lee
NOR DV 445

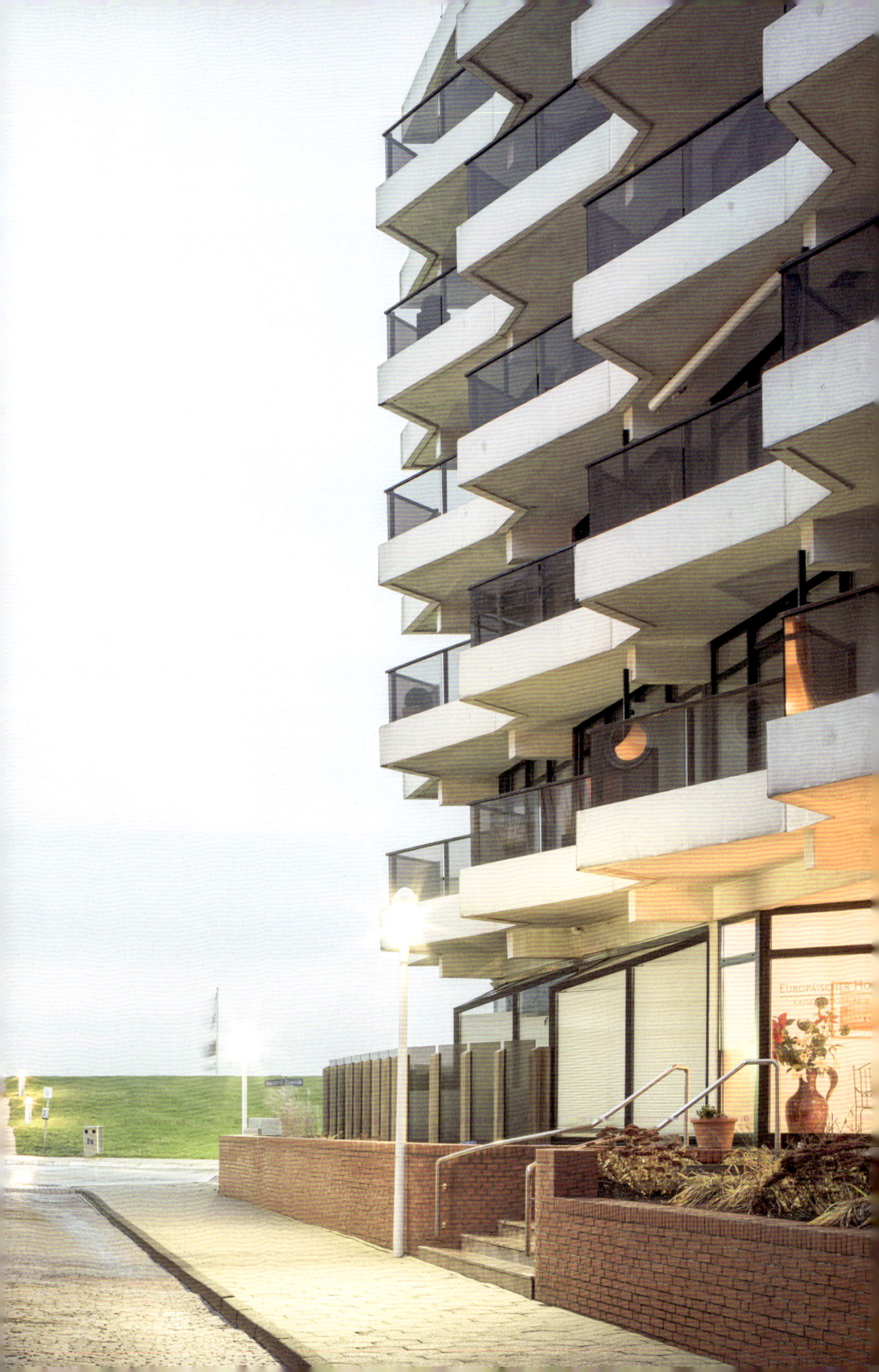
EUROPÄISCHER

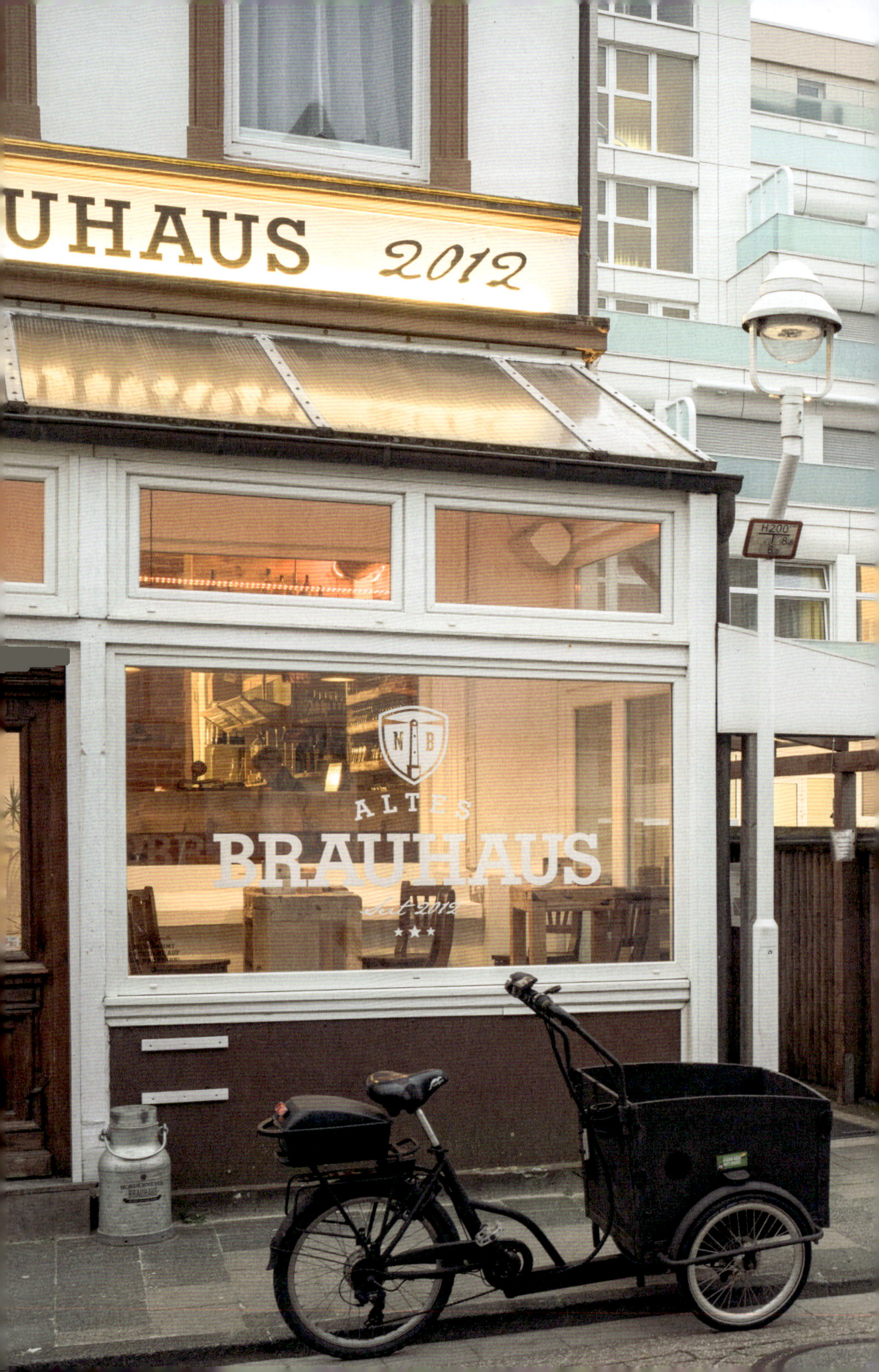
UHAUS 2012
N B
ALTES
BRAUHAUS
seit 2012
H200

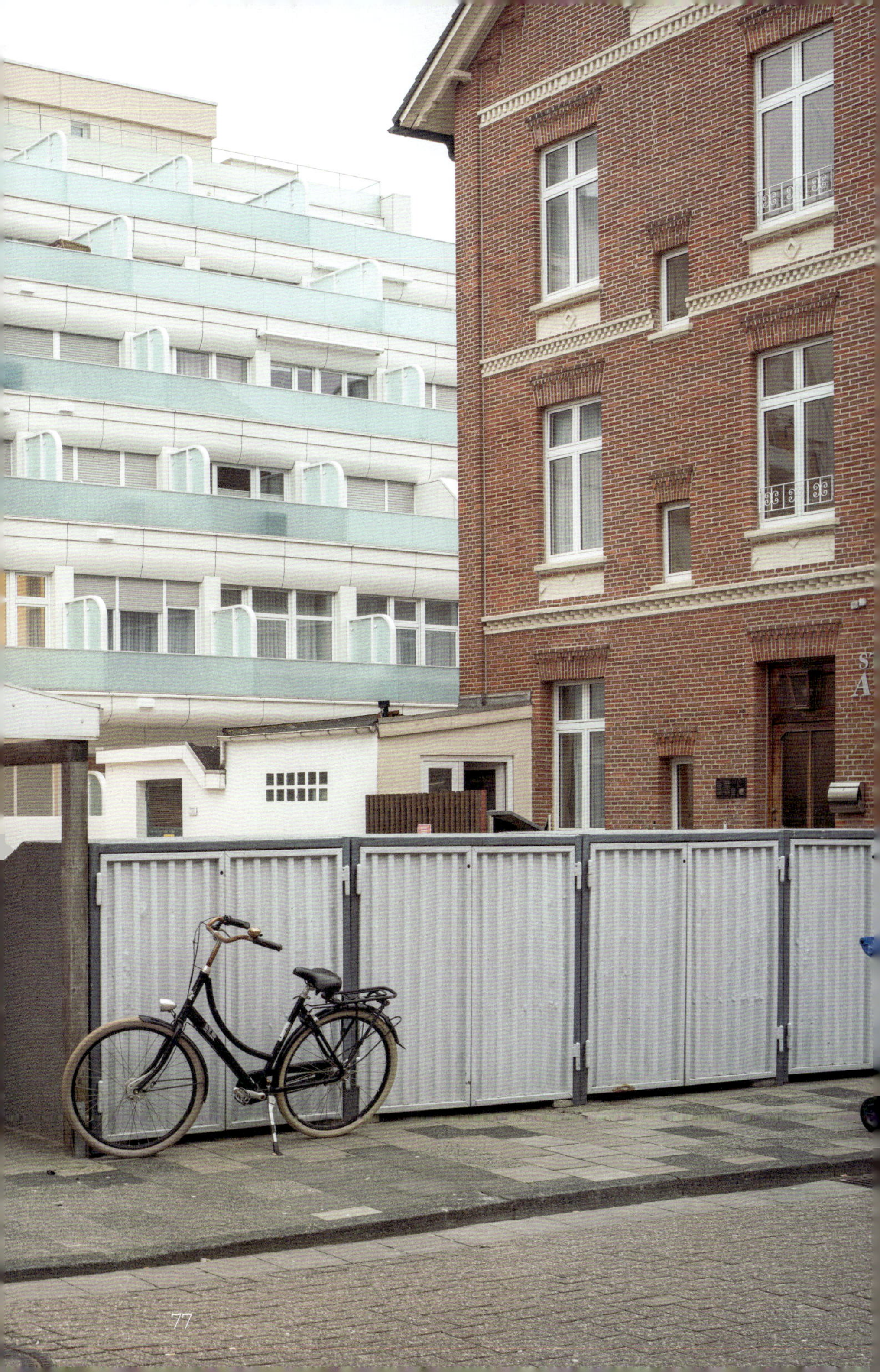

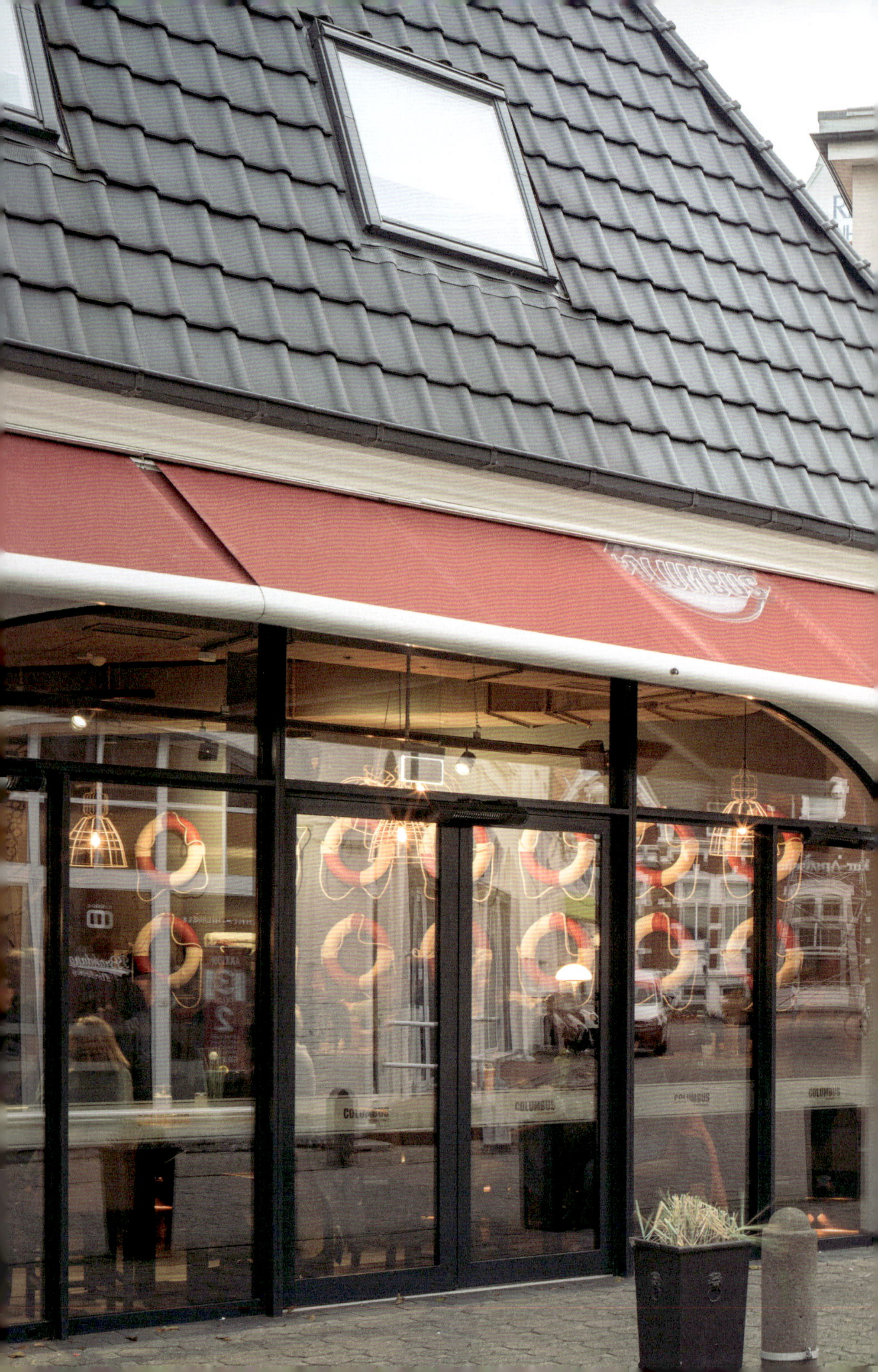
COLUMBUS
COLUMBUS
COLUMBUS
COLUMBUS

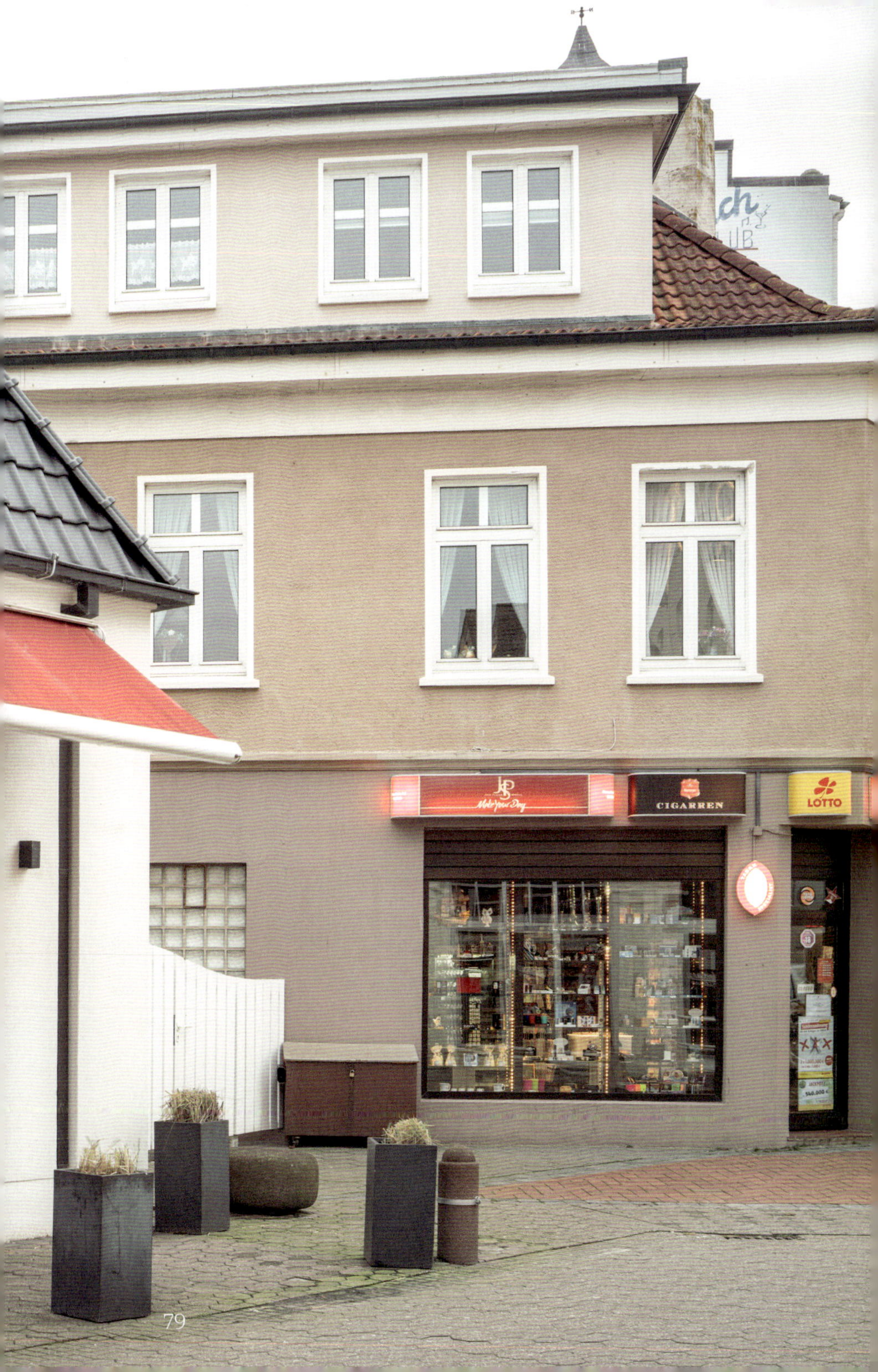
Make Your Day
CIGARREN
LOTTO

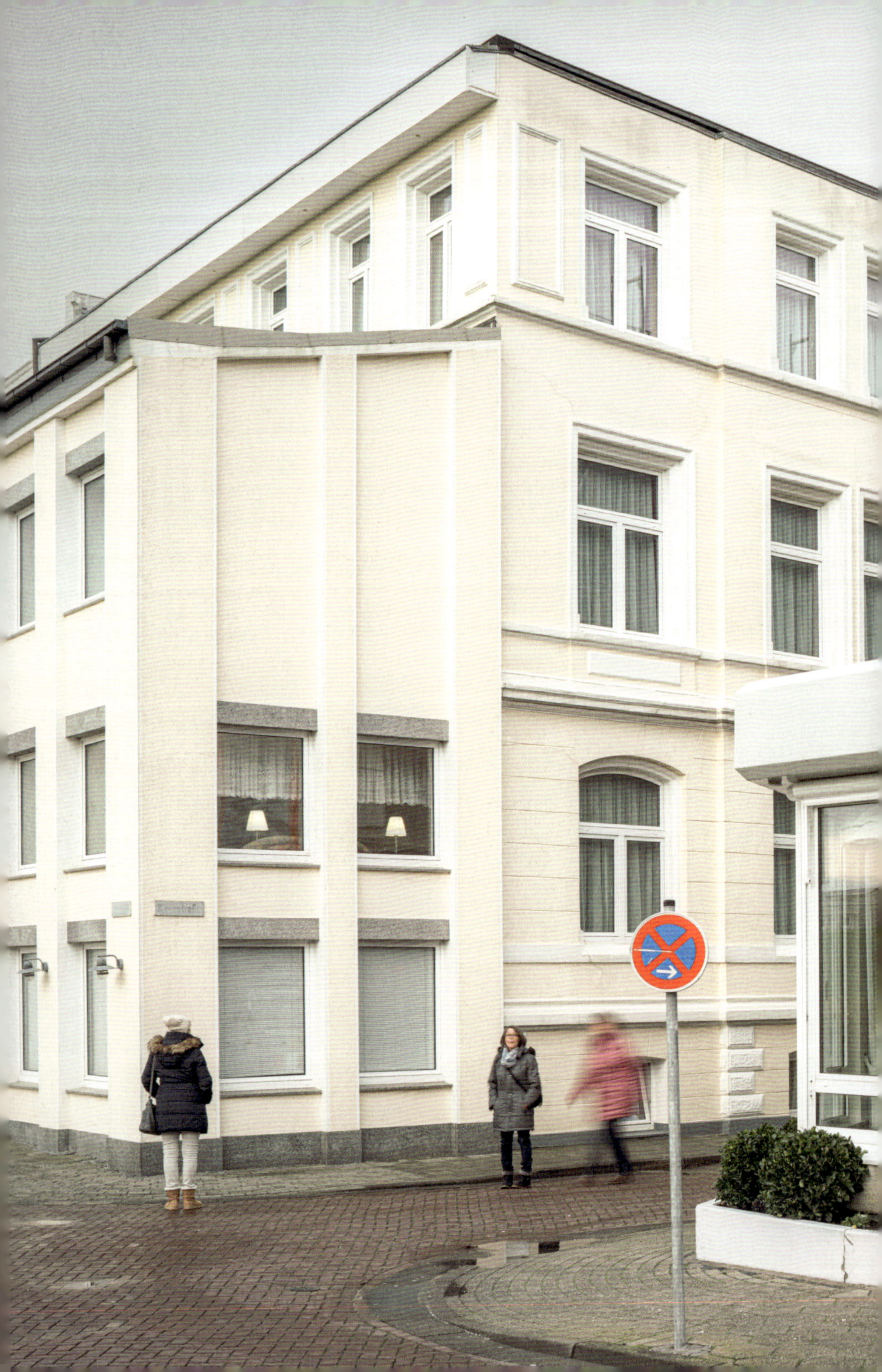

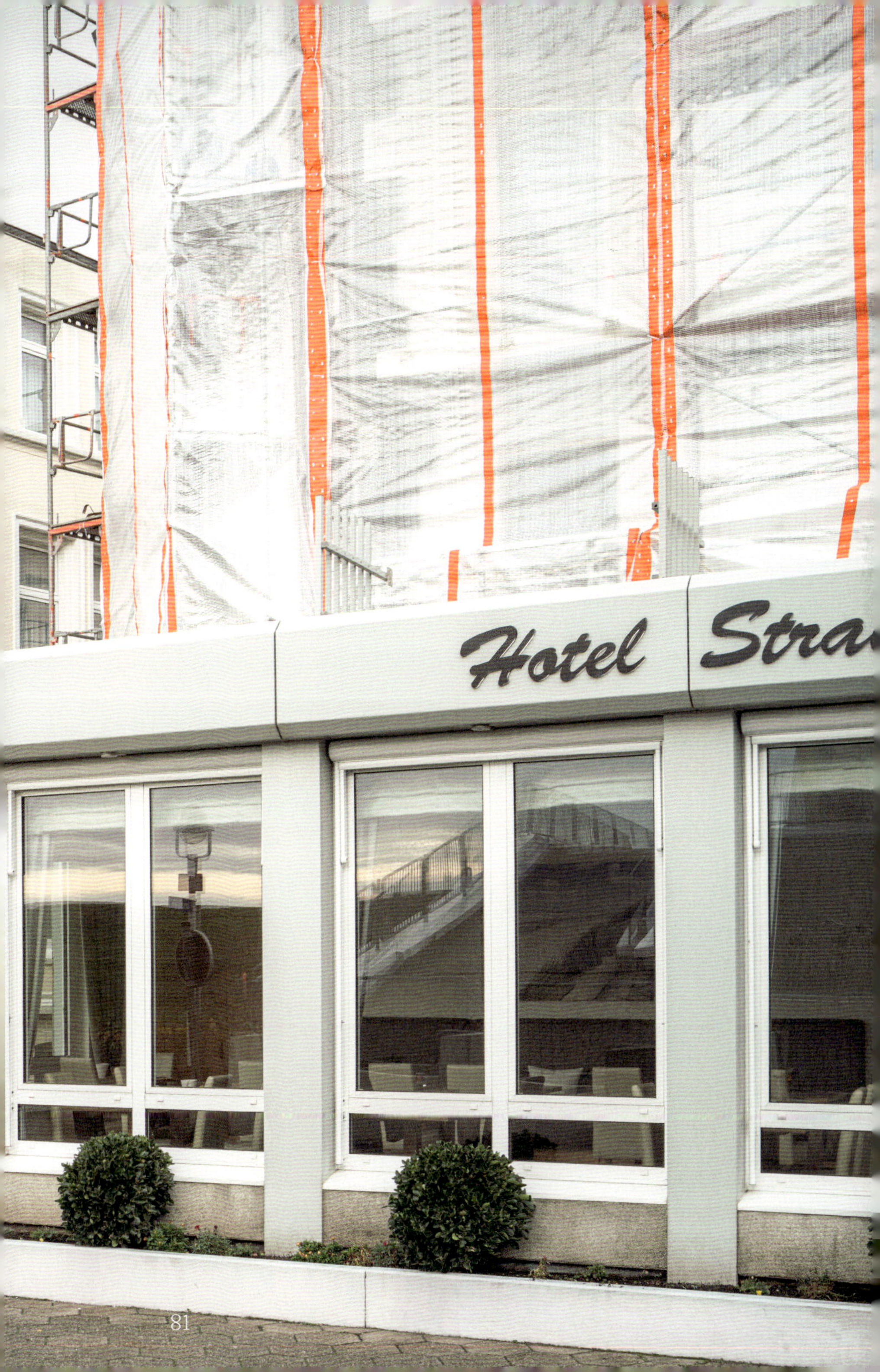
Hotel Stra

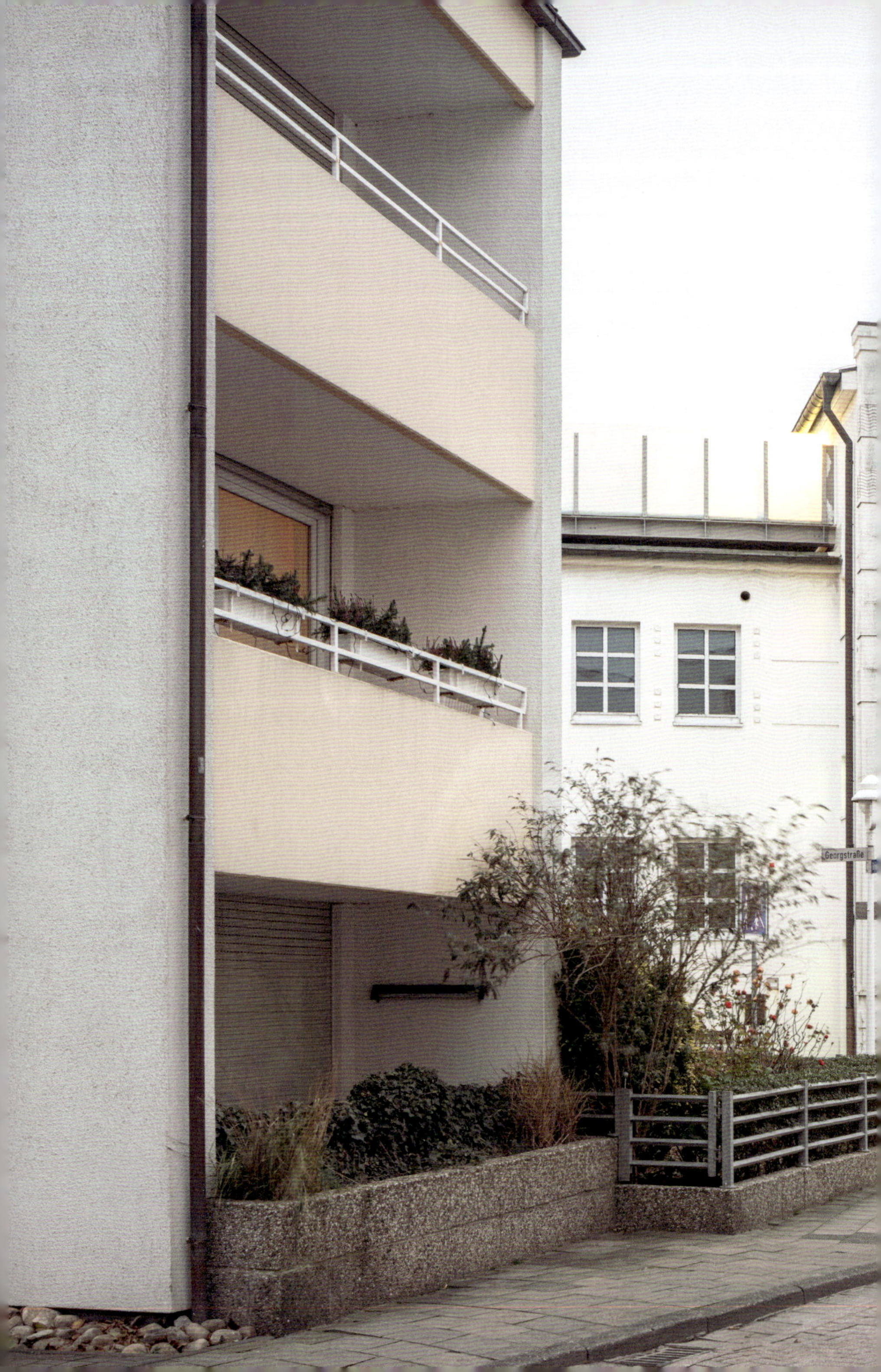
Georgstraße

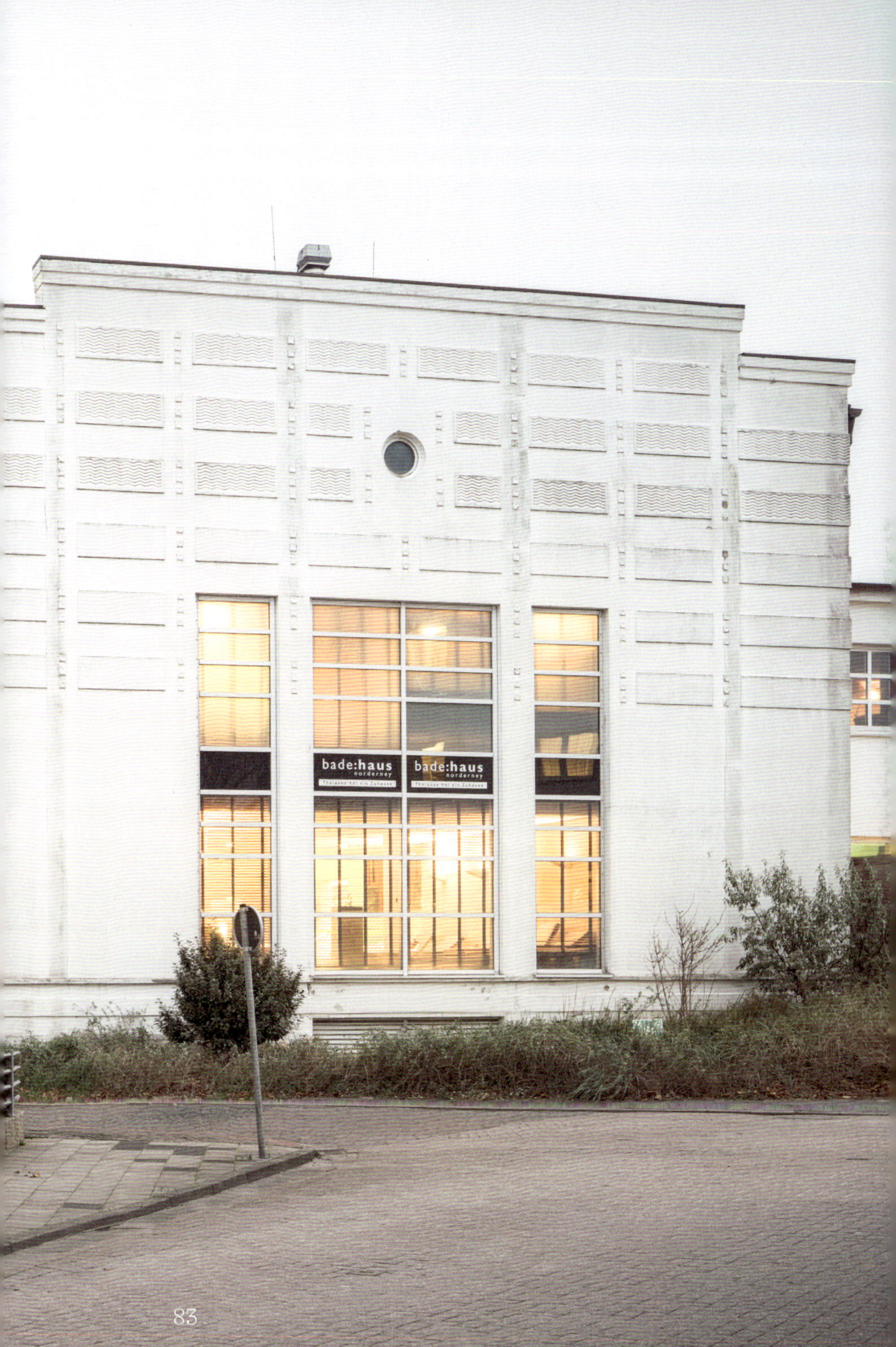
bade:haus
norderney
Thalasso hat ein Zuhause
bade:haus
norderney
Thalasso hat ein Zuhause

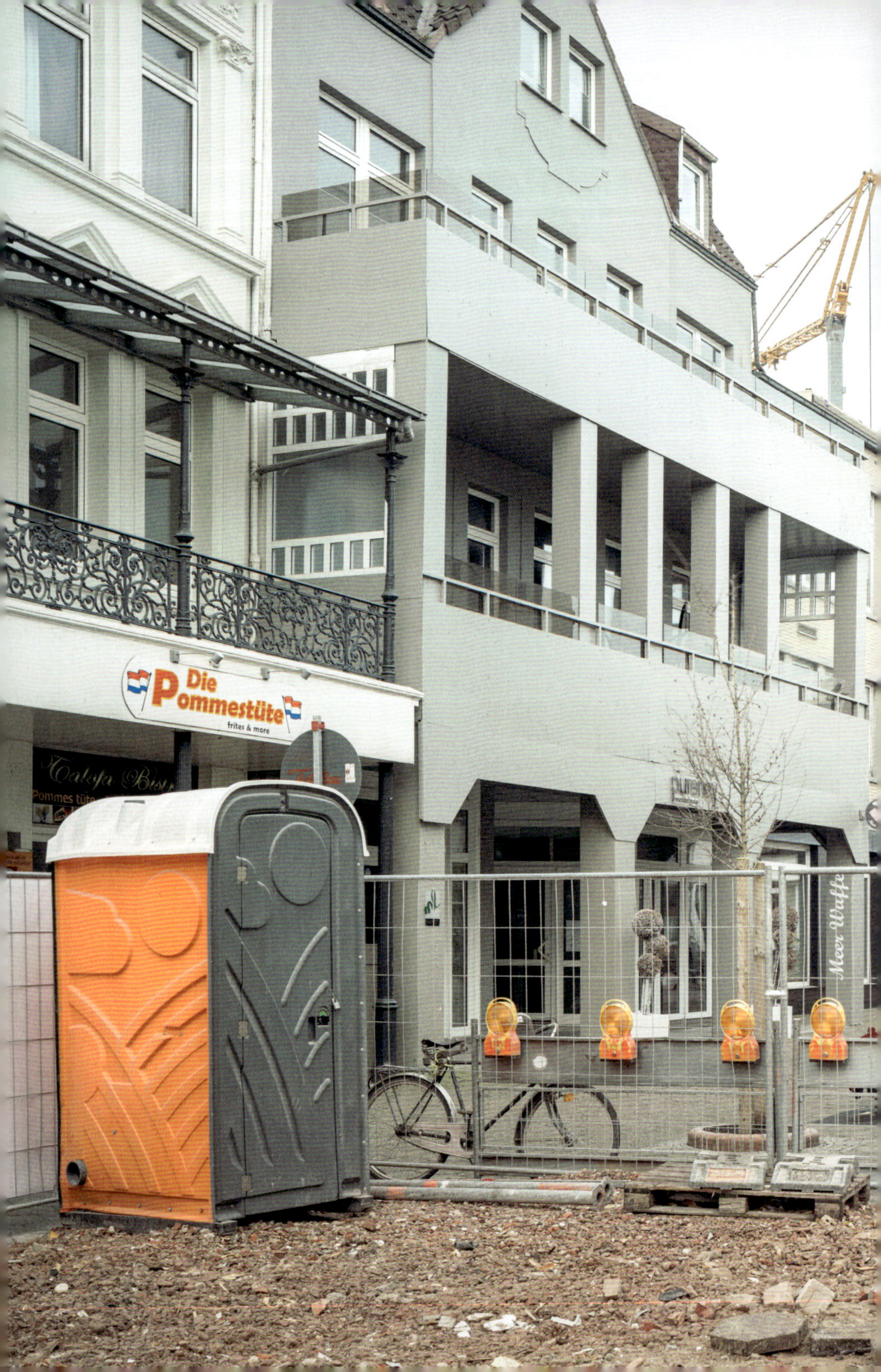
Die
Pommestüte
frites & more

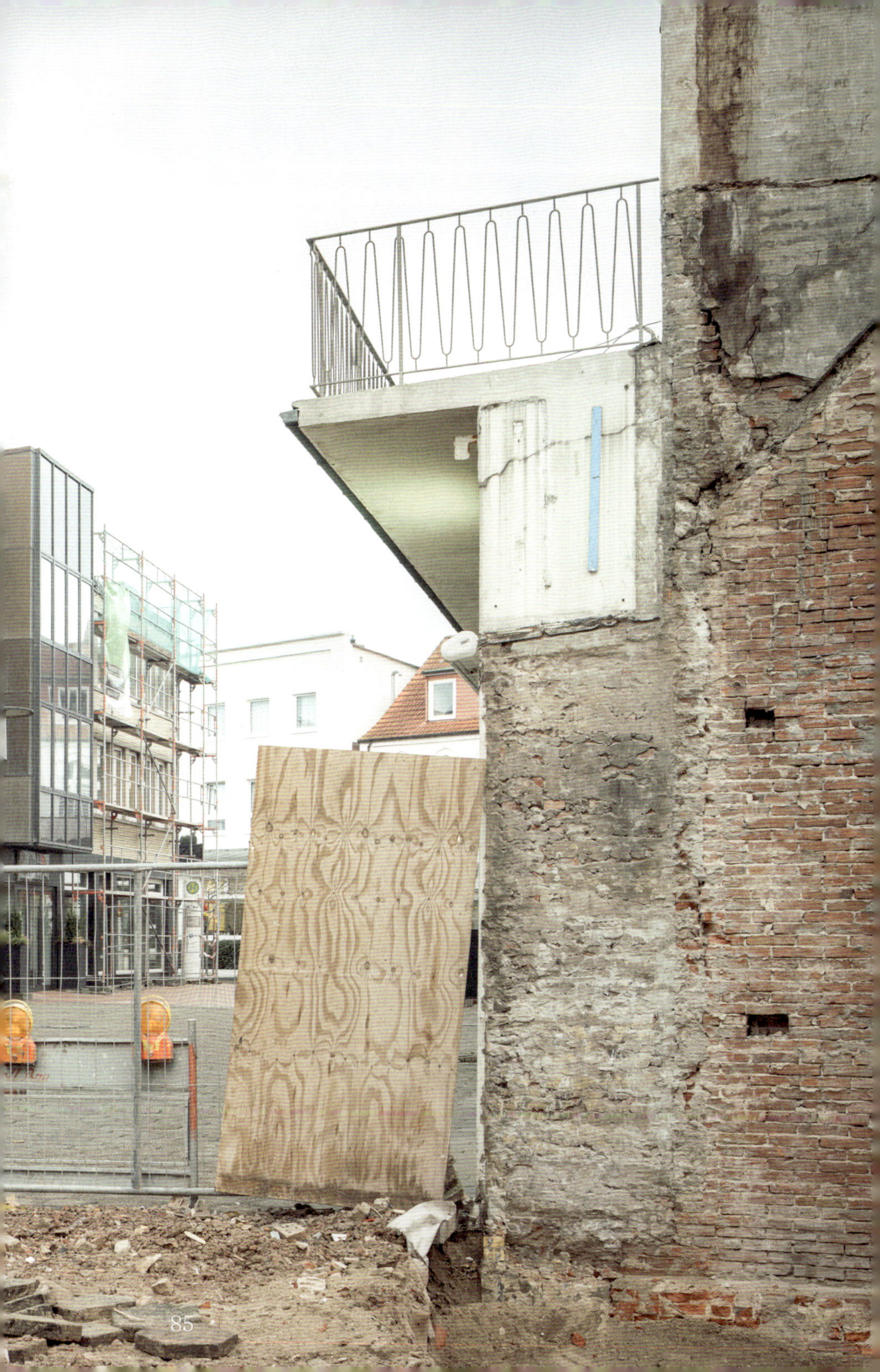

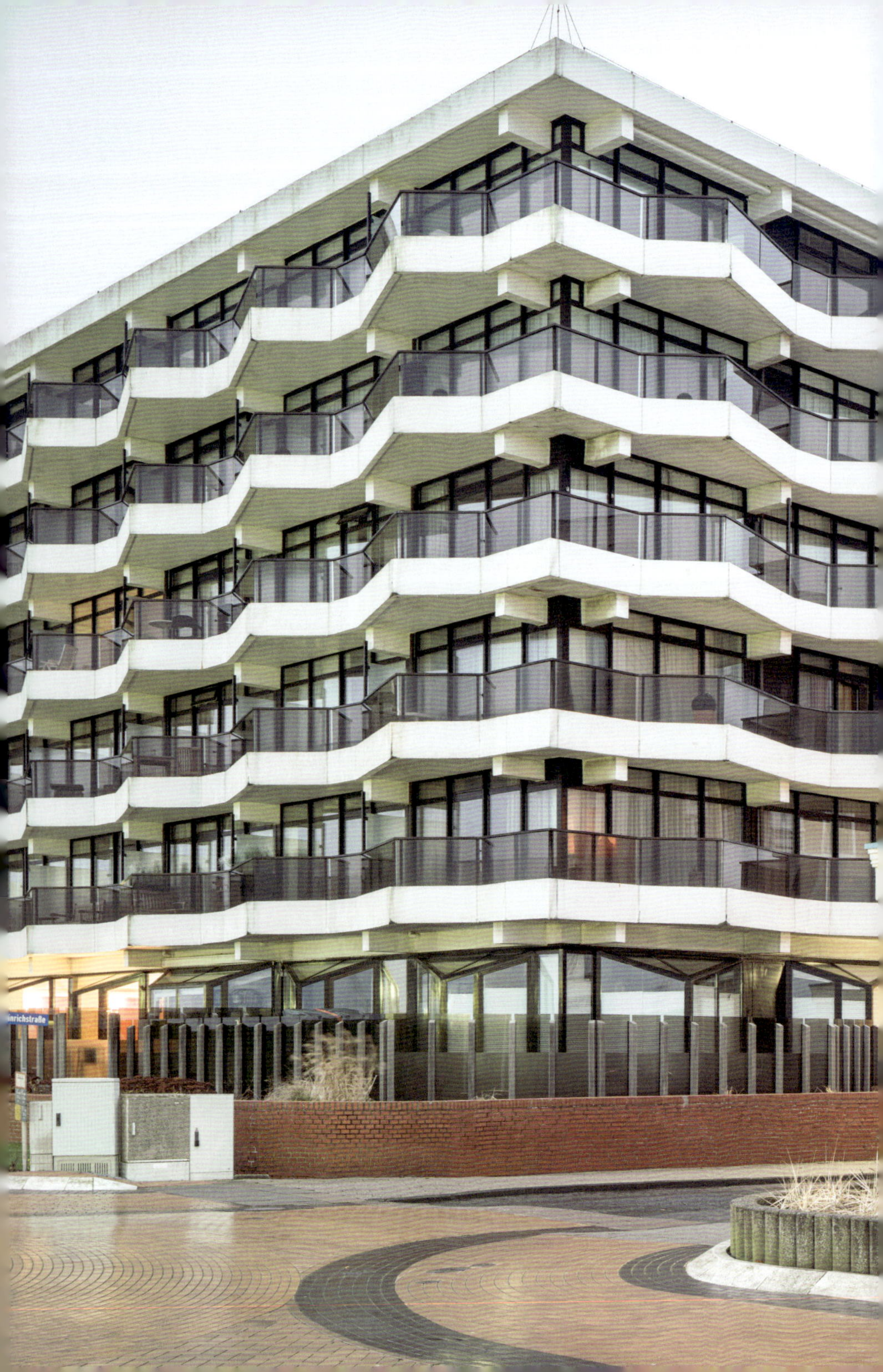
inrichstraße

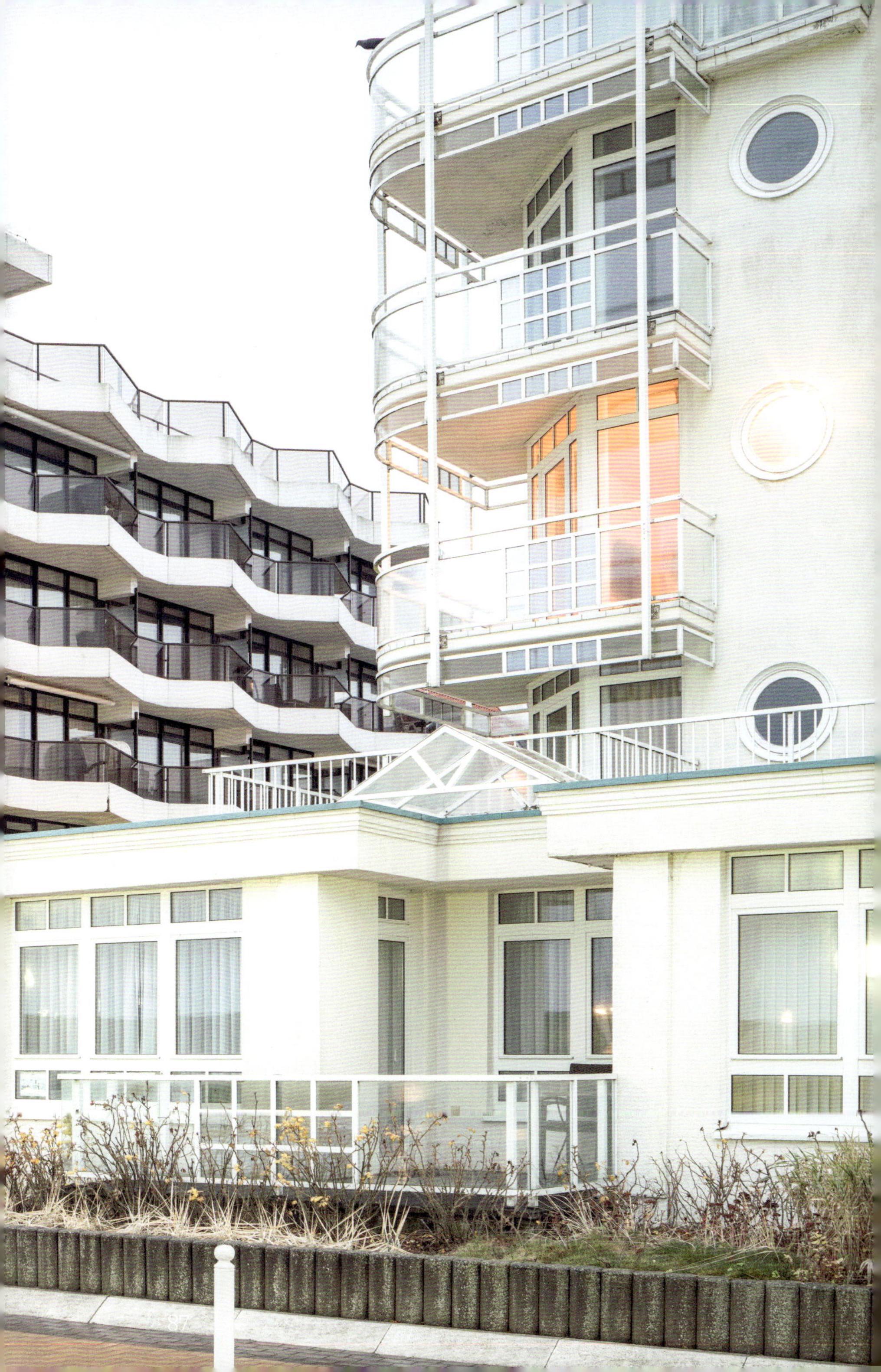

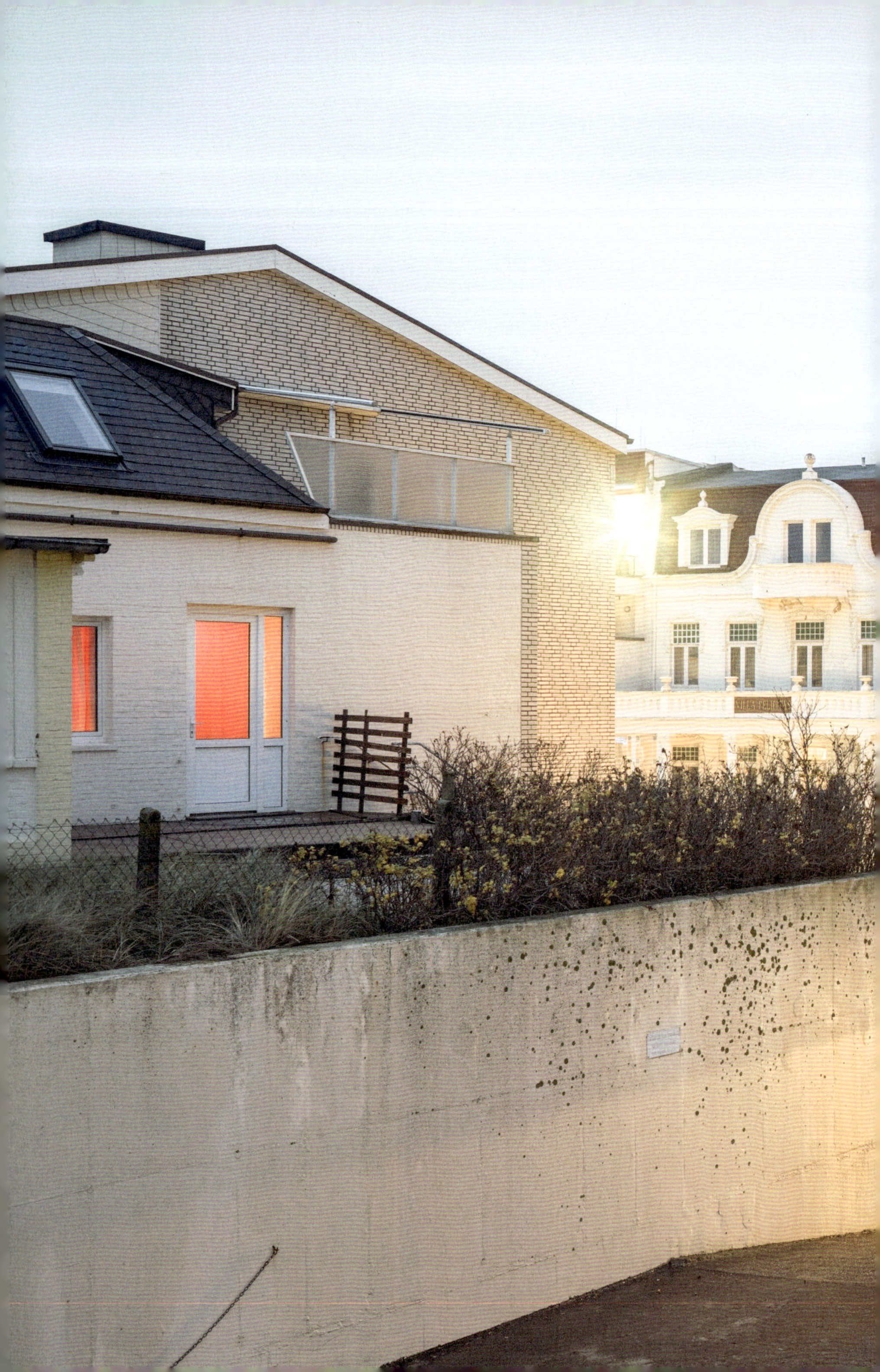

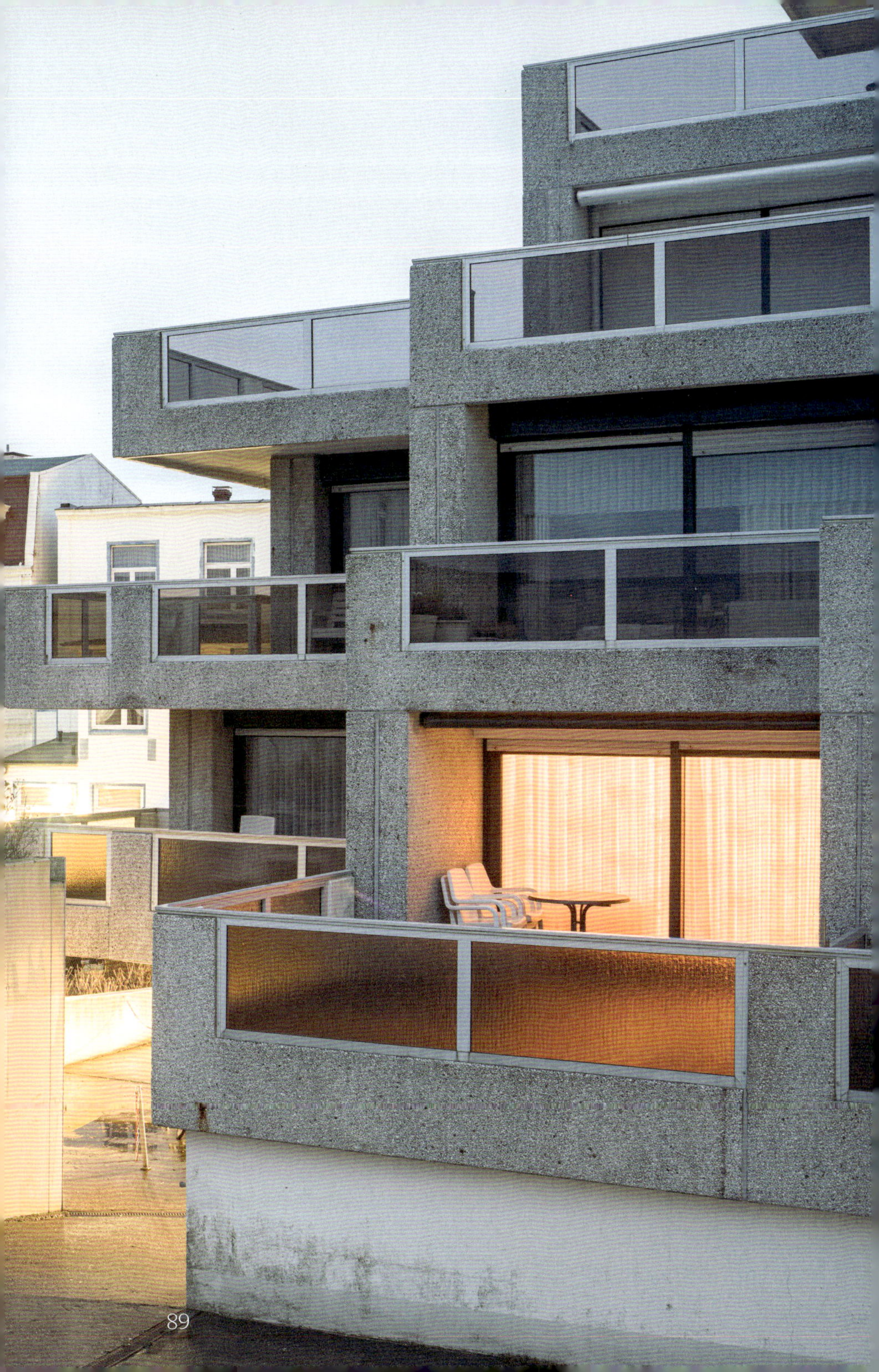

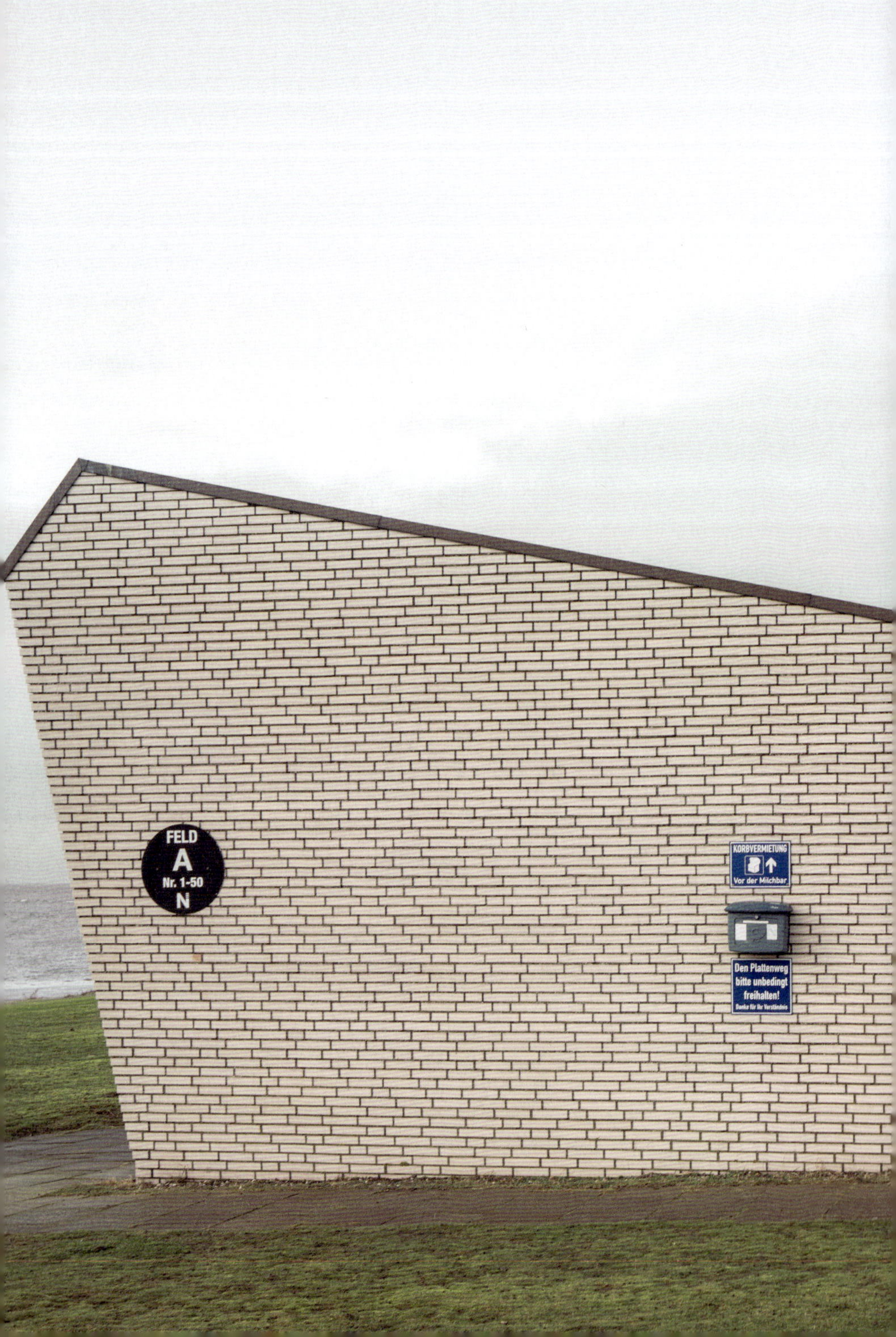
FELD
A
Nr. 1-50
N
KORBVERMIETUNG
Vor der Milchbar
Den Plattenweg
bitte unbedingt
freihalten!
Danke für Ihr Verständnis

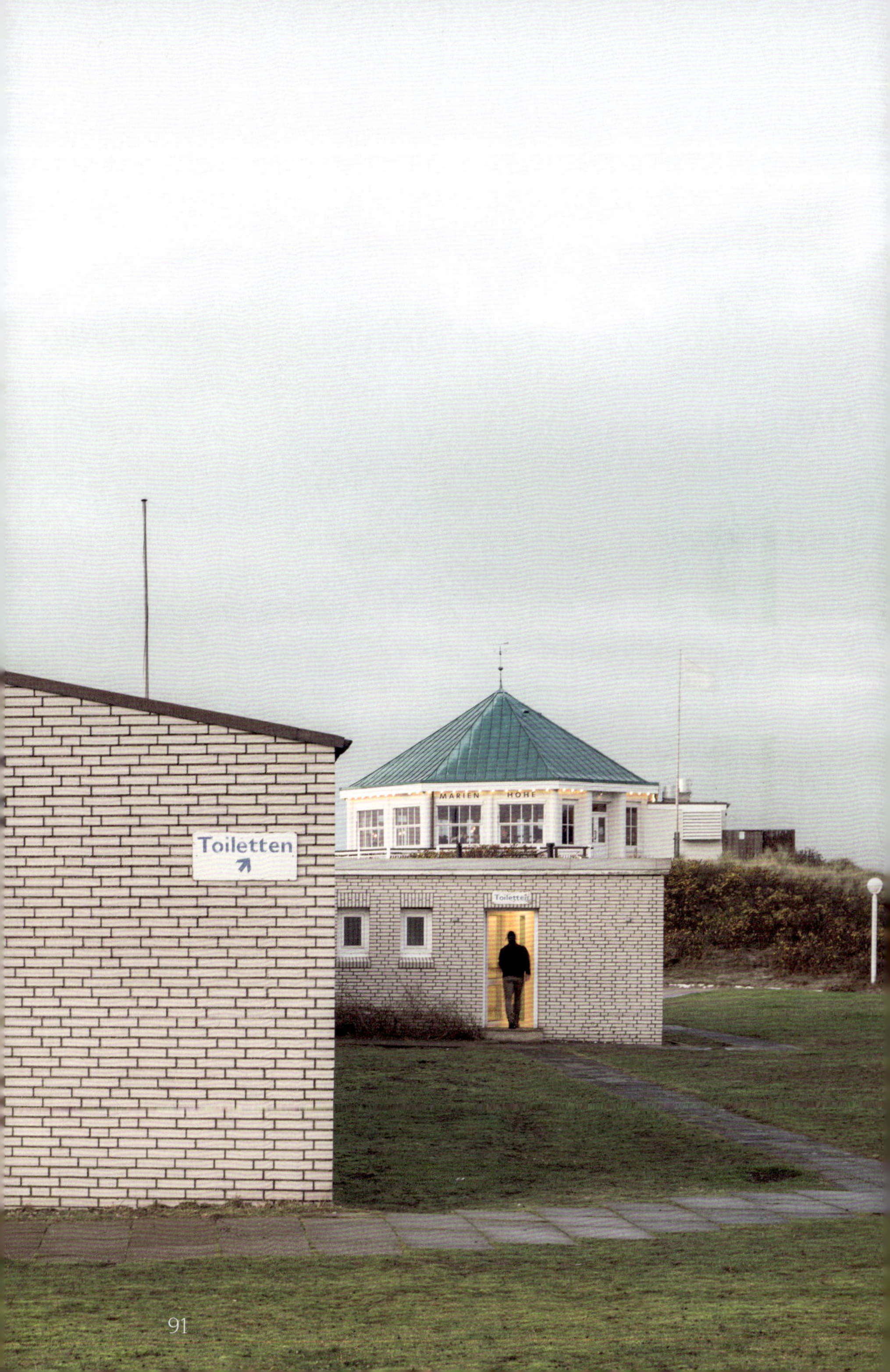
MARIEN HOHE
Toiletten
Toiletten

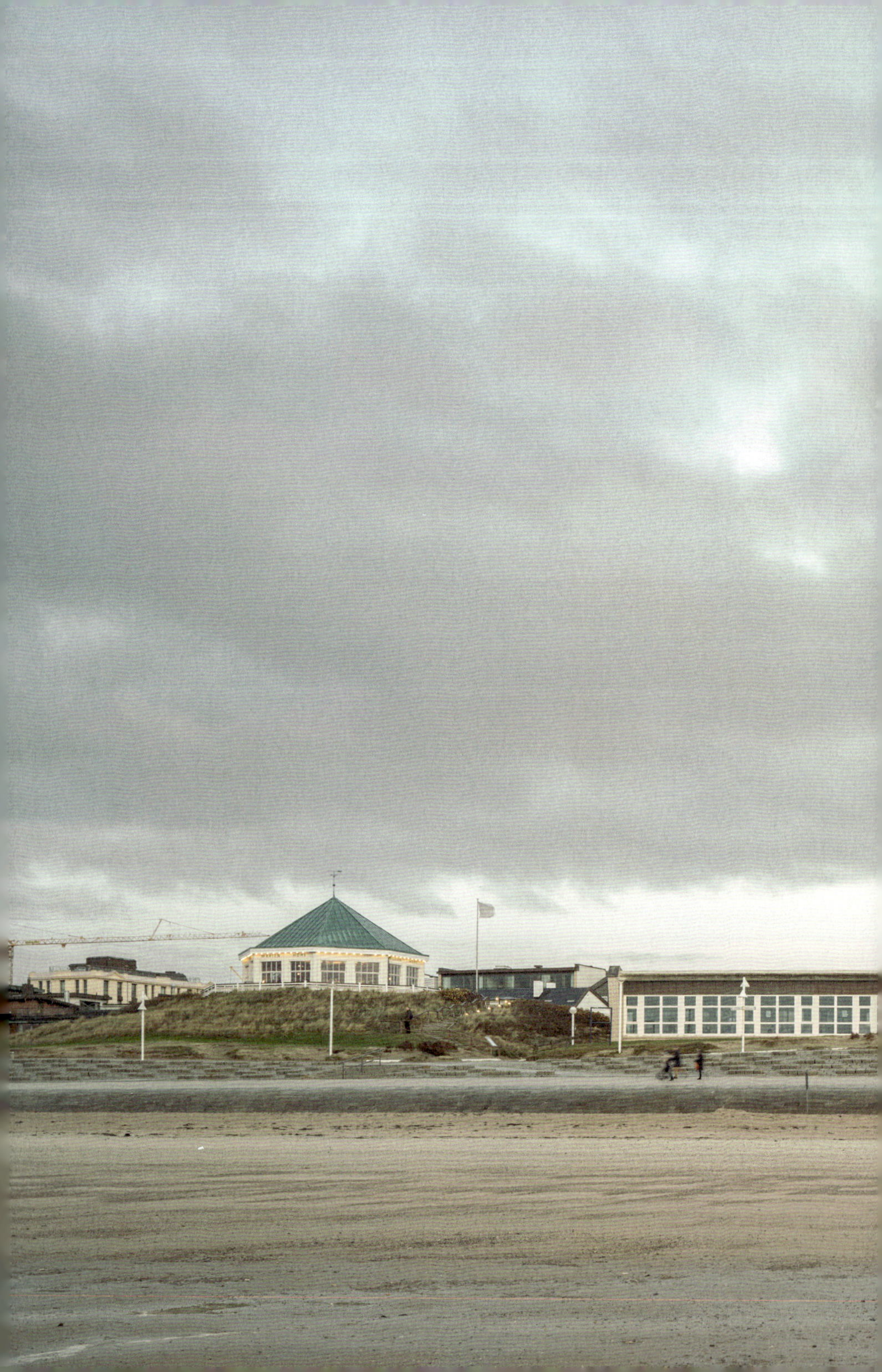

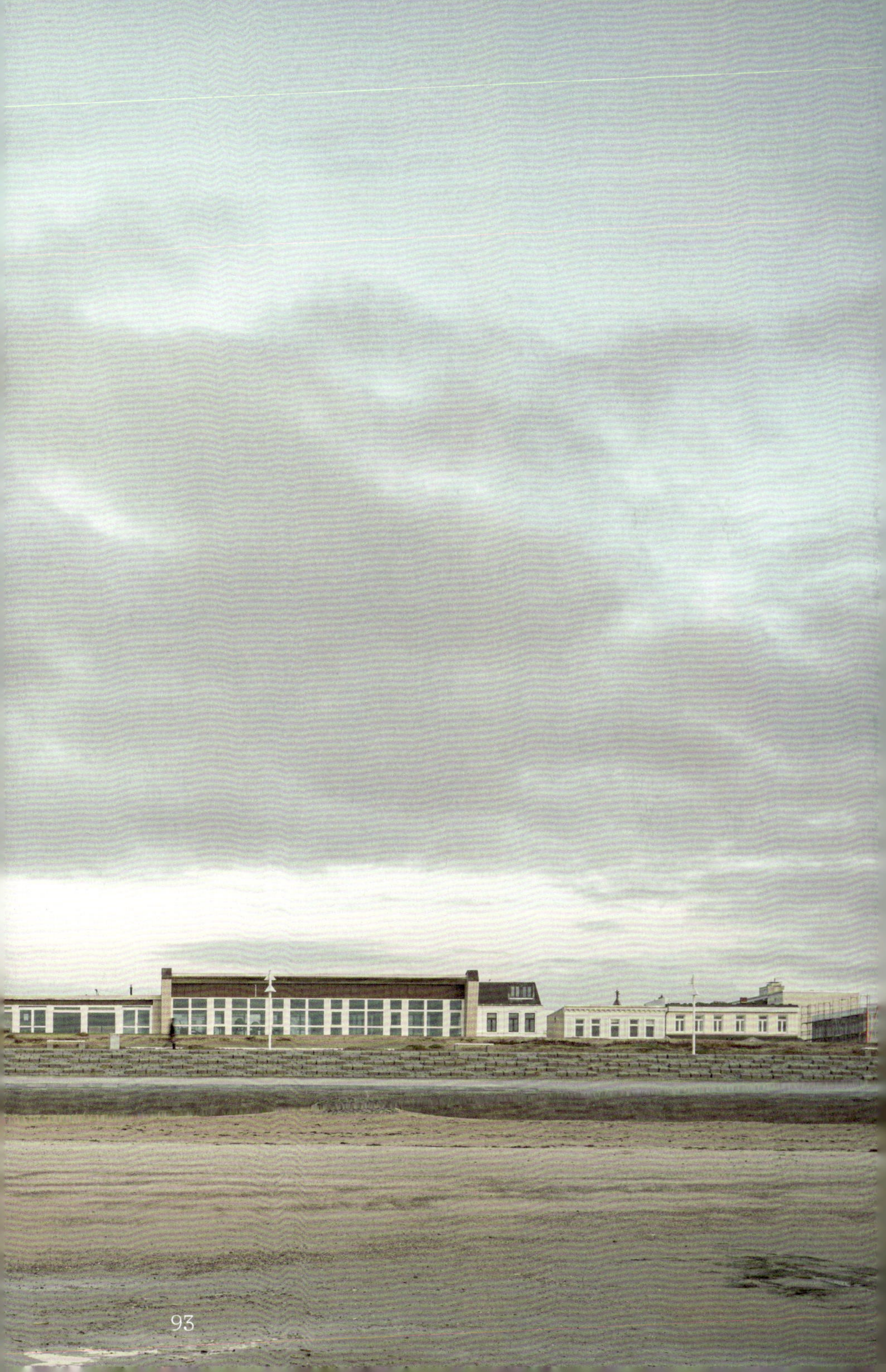

Previous Diaries

Cairo Diary #1
2014
ISBN 978-1-908889-20-1

Athens Diary #2
2015
ISBN 978-1-908889-29-4

Wolfsburg Diary #3
2016
ISBN 978-1-908889-34-8

Taipei Diary #4
2015
ISBN 978-1-908889-30-0

Kochi Diary #5
2018
ISBN 978-1-908889-44-7

Beirut Diary #6
2018
ISBN 978-1-908889-40-9

Wuhan Diary #7
2018
ISBN 978-1-908889-645

Zurich Diary #8
2019
ISBN 978-1-908889-65-2

Budapest Diary #9
2020
ISBN 978-1-908889-66-9

Osaka Diary #10
2020
ISBN 978-1-908889-56-0

Dhaka Diary #11
2021
ISBN 978-1-908889-86-7

Yangon Diary #12
2021
ISBN 978-1-908889-87-4

Minsk Diary #13
2021
ISBN 978-1-908889-88-1

Linz Diary #15
2021
ISBN 978-1-908889-90-4

The diaries listed above were published by *thevelvetcell.com* and are available on the website.

George Town Diary #16
2022
ISBN 978-3-96070-090-6

Unna Diary #17
2022
ISBN 978-3-96070-089-0

Sarajevo Diary #18
2022
ISBN 978-3-96070-088-3

Bangkok Diary #19
2022
ISBN 978-3-96070-087-6

Kuching Diary #20
2024
ISBN 978-3-96070-105-7

Turin Diary #21
2024
ISBN 978-3-96070-103-3

Wilson Diary #22
2024
ISBN 978-3-96070-106-4

London Diary #23
2024
ISBN 978-3-96070-104-0

New York Diary #24
2025
ISBN 978-3-96070-118-7

Vilnius Diary #25
2025
ISBN 978-3-96070-119-4

Istanbul Diary #26
2025
ISBN 978-3-96070-120-0

Norderney Diary #27
2025
ISBN 978-3-96070-121-7

The diaries listed above were published by *hartmann-books.com* and are available on the website.

Norderney Diary
Peter Bialobrzeski

Published by
Hartmann Books
Liststraße 28/1
70180 Stuttgart
info@hartmannprojects.com
hartmann-books.com

Photographs
Peter Bialobrzeski
bialobrzeski.net

Graphic Design and Typesetting
Sarah Fricke, Distaff Studio

Copyediting
Tas Skorupa, New York

Printing and Binding
Gutenberg Beuys, Hannover

Paper
Magno Volume

Typefaces
ABC Diatype, GT Alpina

First Edition, 2025
500 copies

ISBN
978-3-96070-121-7

For Alem